THE
SAXON KINGS

THE
SAXON KINGS

Richard Humble

Introduction by Antonia Fraser

Book Club Associates, London

for my father

© George Weidenfeld and
Nicolson Limited and
Book Club Associates
1980

*First produced in 1980
by George Weidenfeld and
Nicolson Ltd
91 Clapham High Street,
London SW4*

*Picture research by
Faith Perkins
Series designed by
Paul Watkins
Layout by Sheila Sherwen*

*Filmset by Keyspools Limited,
Golborne, Lancashire
Printed in Great Britain
by Morrison and Gibb,
Edinburgh*

Contents

Introduction

THE STORY OF THE CREATION of the Saxon kingdom of England, in the five hundred seething years before the Norman Conquest, is one of the most dramatic tales in our island history; resonant with heroism and victory, as also with treachery and defeat. Not only is the study of it essential to explain our complicated national inheritance – inexplicable if our history is merely held to begin in 1066 with an alien invasion – but these are also centuries rich in interest in their own right; in the course of them an amazing variety of leaders emerges, good and bad, but never remotely dull. Yet all too often the characters of our Saxon kings are ignored in favour of those of their considerably less startling Norman successors.

It is a story which does of course contain some names well known in popular legends, such as Arthur and Alfred. The 'real' King Arthur was a somewhat shadowy figure (although he did feature in Romano-British resistance to the Germanic invasions of the fifth century). The ninth-century Alfred of Wessex, on the other hand, proves on closer inspection to justify totally his heroic status – fighting 'like a wild boar' against the Danes at Ashdown, keeping the spark of national honour alive during his 'finest hour' as a fugitive on the isle of Athelney, and later, as king of the English in all but the name, tranforming the old notion of a warrior king into something more majestic.

In other cases the Saxon leaders turn out to have been labelled quite incorrectly in our mythology: Ethelred 'the Unready' only acquired that description after his death, and is better summed up by his contemporary nickname of 'Evil-Counsel'; Edward 'the Confessor' on the other hand was by no means the pious greybeard of tradition, but rather a past master in the one essential Saxon royal art – survival. Most striking of all, perhaps, is the true character of Canute, no foolish sea-defying monarch, but, on the contrary, a happy surprise for the English: a Dane who pursued a policy of reconciliation with his English subjects, animated by a respect for English institutions.

Then there are Saxon kings unjustly neglected, such as Edward the Elder, who as 'King of the Anglo-Saxons' took his people on to the national offensive against the Danes, and expanded their boundaries until, after fifteen years of brilliant and relentless reconquest, by 924 he had secured a united realm. Yet, as Richard Humble points out, this glorious 'English Reconquest' remains sunk in oblivion, although even the Scots acknowledged the stature of Edward by choosing him as their lord.

Above all this is the remarkable story of the emergence of a national identity, from the far-off days of Aelle, the first King of the South Saxons (or Sussex), down to the defeat of Harold Godwinesson at Hastings. Interwoven with it is the progress, often erratic, of Christianity in England, and the growth of English civilization and culture; while Norse predators of varying degrees of ferocity chequer the tale with their assaults on our shores. In a narrative which is both clear and compelling, Richard Humble inspires a new excitement concerning our Saxon heritage.

Antonia Fraser

Acknowledgments

Photographs and illustrations are supplied or reproduced by kind permission of the following: Antikvarisk-Topografiska Arkivet, Stockholm 43 (photo Soren Hallgren); Ashmolean Museum 54, 63, 170 *Weidenfeld and Nicolson Archives*; BBC Hulton Picture Library 93, 118–19, 123, 142, 148, 150, 154 left and right, 156–7, 178–9, 184, 186; Bibliothèque Municipale, Le Mans 111; Bodleian Library 4–5, 15, 16, 126, 138 top, 166, 167, 212–3; 24–5, 58–9, 73, 76, 91 *Weidenfeld and Nicolson Archives*; Janet and Colin Bord 35; British Library 2; British Museum 3, 11, 14, 26–7, 29, 32, 80–1, 84 right, 96–7, 100, 112–13, 116–17, 121, 136–7, 146, 153, 169, 184–5, 202 *Weidenfeld and Nicolson Archives*; 204–5 BPC; 207, 209 *John Topham*; Bundesdenkmalamt, Vienna 84 left *Weidenfeld and Nicolson Archives*; Cambridge University Library endpapers, 178–9, 189 *BBC Hulton Picture Library*; Masters and Fellows of Corpus Christi College, Cambridge 87, 94, 132–3; Department of the Environment (Crown copyright) 37 *Weidenfeld and Nicolson Archives*; Mary Evans Picture Library 21, 183; Sonia Halliday 161; Michael Holford 124–5 (photo Ianthe Ruthven), 195, 198, 199; James A. Irving 139; A. F. Kersting 174, 175; Laing Art Gallery 164–5; London Museum 68, 106 top and bottom *Weidenfeld and Nicolson Archives*; Manchester City Council 22 *Mansell Collection*, 64–5 *BBC Hulton Picture Library*; Mansell Collection 38–9, 56–7, 128, 130, 197; National Trust 28; Photoresources 194; Popperfoto 17; Science Museum 138 bottom; Ronald Sheridan 41; Library of Trinity College, Dublin 33; Universitetets Oldsaksamling, Oslo 69 *Weidenfeld and Nicolson Archives*; Weidenfeld and Nicolson Archives 34, 190–1.

Numbers in italics refer to colour illustrations.

Maps and family trees by Heather Sherratt.
Picture research by Faith Perkins.

1 The Seven

Kingdoms

I T IS ODD THAT SUCH OBSCURITY still shrouds the rulers of Saxon England. Their figures loom vaguely through a fog-bank of history cut short, with ruthless clarity, by that most baneful of dates: 1066. 'Willy, Willy, Harry, Ste; Harry, Dick, John, Harry Three' – the kings who ruled England 'before the Conquest' are ruthlessly omitted from this famous schoolroom *aide-memoire*. Why, for instance, is the thirteenth-century ruler Edward Plantagenet always known as Edward I, though there were three kings of England before him of the same name?

For every ten people who can recite the succession of England's rulers from William I to Elizabeth II, there is probably not one who can do the same for the Saxon kings from Alfred to Harold. Considering that the former group of monarchs takes up a full nine centuries and the above-mentioned Saxon kings only a century and a half, this is surely peculiar. And considering that the Saxon kings from Alfred to Harold *created* the kingdom of England – for such an entity had not existed before Alfred's time – this comparative neglect becomes downright inexcusable. In 1066 the conquering Normans were historical parvenus, with their small and embattled homeland precariously ruled by warlords who claimed no title loftier than duke; but the English had been ruled by kings for over five centuries. They were intensely proud of this tradition, which was put in writing and kept for posterity by the invaluable document known as the *Anglo-Saxon Chronicle*.

Written up over the centuries in Old (Saxon) English by monks of the Church, the *Chronicle* is a peculiar hybrid, often cheerfully blending pride in the memory of pagan ancestors with Christian piety. This is the conclusion of the *Chronicle* entry recording the death of King Aethelwulf, father of Alfred 'the Great', in 858:

And Aethelwulf was the son of Egbert, the son of Ealhmund, the son of Eafa, the son of Eoppa, the son of Ingild. Ingild was the brother of Ine, king of the West Saxons, who held the kingdom for 37 years and afterwards went to St Peter's and ended his life there. And they were sons of Cenred. Cenred was the son of Ceolwold, the son of Cutha, the son of Cuthwine, the son of Ceawlin, the son of Cynric, the son of Creoda, the son of Cerdic. Cerdic was the son of Elesa, the son of Esla, the son of Gewis, the son of Wig, the son of

PREVIOUS PAGES Hinged gold and enamel buckle with interlaced ornamentation, from the early seventh-century grave (probably that of Raedwald of East Anglia) at Sutton Hoo.

12

Freawine, the son of Freothogar, the son of Brand, the son of Baeldaeg, the son of Woden, the son of Frealaf, the son of Finn, the son of Godwulf, the son of Geat, the son of Taetwa, the son of Beaw, the son of Sceldwa, the son of Heremod, the son of Itermon, the son of Hathra, the son of Hwala, the son of Bedwig, the son of Sceaf, i.e. the son of Noah. He was born in Noah's Ark. Lamech, Methuselah, Enoch, Jared, Mahalaleel, Cainan, Enos, Seth, Adam the first man and our father, i.e. Christ. Amen.

Together, the seven surviving manuscripts of the *Chronicle* trace the Saxon kings right back to the fifth and early sixth centuries AD. Mind-boggling genealogies such as the one quoted above are mercifully rare in the *Chronicle*, which insists that the first English kingdoms were founded by three Germanic peoples known as the Jutes, the Saxons and the Angles:

> From the Jutes came the people of Kent and of the Isle of Wight, namely the tribe which now inhabits the Isle of Wight and that race in Wessex which is still called the race of the Jutes. From the Old Saxons came the East Saxons, the South Saxons and the West Saxons. From Angeln, which afterwards remained waste, between the Jutes and the Saxons, came the East Angles, the Middle Angles, the Mercians and all the Northumbrians.

The *Chronicle* asserts that around 450 AD Jutish warriors led by the brothers Hengest and Horsa were invited across the Channel by Vortigern, ruler of the hard-pressed and totally isolated former Roman province of Britain. Vortigern summoned the Jutes to fight as mercenaries against the savage Picts of the north, but once the Picts were beaten the Jutes refused to leave: 'They then sent to Angeln, bidding them send more help, and had them informed of the cowardice of the Britons and the excellence of the land.'

The Jutish wars of conquest lasted some thirty years, starting with victory over Vortigern's troops in two pitched battles (455 and 456) which forced the British to abandon Kent. Horsa was killed in the first battle, leaving Hengest and his son Aesc as the war-leaders of the Jutes. Though no mention is made of the year Hengest died, in 488 'Aesc succeeded to the kingdom and was king of the people of Kent for twenty-four years'. By the end of the fifth century, the first of the English kingdoms was clearly established.

Hengest was almost certainly still alive and leading the Jutes

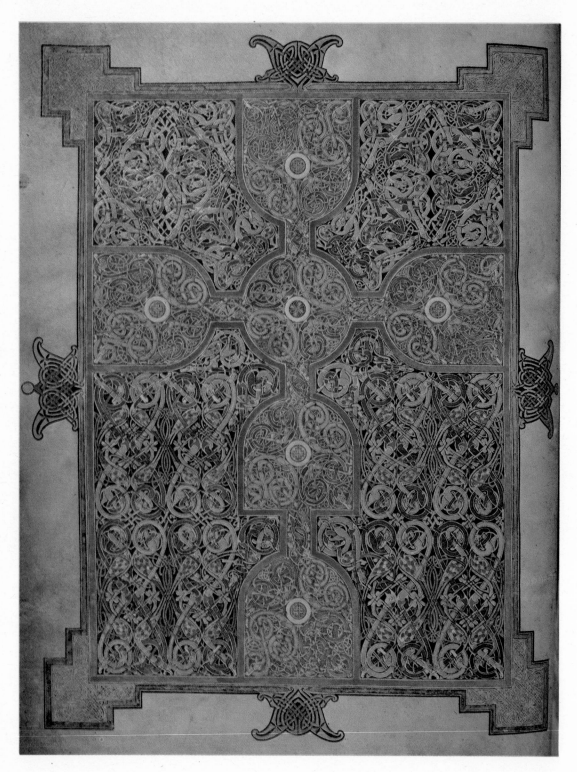

14

ABOVE St Cuthbert, patron saint of Northumbria, appears to Alfred of Wessex – a good example of how the Christian faith served as an early bond between the disparate kingdoms of north and south.

OPPOSITE The 'Carpet page' of the *Lindisfarne Gospels*, illuminated by Edfrith, Bishop of Lindisfarne (698–721).

of Kent when the first Saxons began a war of conquest in 477. In that year the chieftain Aelle, with his sons Cymen, Wlencing, and Cissa, landed on the south coast near Selsey Bill. They set about conquering the coastal strip of Sussex – the new 'kingdom of the South Saxons' – between the coast and the then impenetrable Weald Forest. Aelle, the first king of Sussex, was clearly a formidable war leader. In 491 his men stormed the British fortress of Pevensey ('Anderida' to the Romano-British, 'Andredesceaster' to the Saxons) and massacred all the British within its mighty walls.

Four years later, in 495, Cerdic and his son Cynric landed further west along the coast, at the head of Southampton

ABOVE Pevensey, whose massive outer walls were stormed by Aelle's warriors in 491.

OPPOSITE The coastal fortresses of Roman Britain's 'Saxon Shore' in the last years of the province, from the medieval *Notitia Dignitatum*.

Water, possibly, and launched the Saxon invasion north into Hampshire and Wiltshire, an area that grew into the kingdom of the West Saxons: Wessex. The *Chronicle* records Cerdic as dying in 534, succeeded by Cynric, and thirteen years after Cerdic's death a fourth kingdom was founded north of the Humber by the Anglian chieftain Ida, who set up a fortified base at Bamburgh, heartland of the kingdom of Northumbria.

Such is the bare outline of how the Anglo-Saxon conquest of Britain began, as recorded centuries after the event by the *Chronicle*. It is far from complete, making no reference to the coming of the East Angles, East Saxons, Middle Saxons, Middle Angles or Mercians. Nor does the *Chronicle* admit that between about 500 and 545 the invaders seem to have been halted by the last great resistance of the Romano-Britons, under a shadowy leader who lays the best claim to having been the 'real' King Arthur. It took Cynric of Wessex until 552 to beat the British at Salisbury, while Cynric's son Ceawlin only took Gloucester and Bath in 577. But for all its shortcomings as a historical document, the *Chronicle* contains several important clues to the nature of pagan Anglo-Saxon kingship by the close of the sixth century.

The king's most obvious duty during the wars of conquest was to win victory in battle. Only by repeated conquest could he hope to keep his warriors safely occupied and supplied with spoil – both of the portable variety and in the form of land conquered from the king's enemies. The royal title normally passed from father to son, the heir-apparent being his father's right-hand man from an early stage. It was clearly in the son's interest to prove himself the most promising candidate for the kingship during his years of parental tutelage, for too many likely candidates in the royal family invariably resulted in a disputed succession. The confusing sequence of entries in the *Chronicle* suggests that Cerdic and Cynric of Wessex had to deal with such competition from 'their two kinsmen', Stuf and Wihtgar, who eventually accepted the Isle of Wight and left Cerdic and Cynric to rule the West Saxons on the mainland.

The kingdom with the biggest succession problem was Northumbria. Ida of Northumbria, the first king, died in 560 but his son Aethelric did not succeed him, probably because he was too young. The new king was 'Aelle the son of Yffe', whose

18

twenty-eight-year reign kept Aethelric from the Northumbrian throne until 588. Aethelric's son Aethelfrith succeeded in 593, but the heirs of Aelle provided a rival ruling line which split Northumbria and implanted a fateful tradition of civil war in the kingdom.

Though all the Saxon kings claimed common descent from Woden, lord of the gods, this was merely one of the standard trappings of royal dignity and was no bar to wars between neighbouring kingdoms. The first recorded war between the southern kingdoms took the form of an assault by Ceawlin of Wessex on Ethelbert of Kent in 568, at a place which the *Chronicle* calls 'Wibbandun'. This may have been Westerham, on the west Kentish border, suggesting a West Saxon march east along the ridge of the North Downs to teach the Kentishmen who were masters. It was not an attempt to conquer Kent, for although Ethelbert was driven back into his kingdom he suffered no further attacks from Ceawlin.

Ceawlin's own story is one of the biggest enigmas of the sixth century. He was easily the dominant war-leader of the age, shattering the British defensive perimeter in the south and driving deep into central England. But Ceawlin's father Cynric seems to have anticipated the error of Henry Plantagenet 600 years later and produced too many sons for his kingdom's comfort. Apart from Ceawlin, the West Saxons were also apparently led by the King's brothers, Cutha and Cuthwulf, between 568 and 584. Ceawlin's reign ended in 592 when he was 'driven out' after a great slaughter; he 'perished', together with Cwichelm and Crida (probably his own sons) in the following year. It took another five years before Ceawlin's nephew Ceolwulf, the son of Cutha, emerged as undisputed king of Wessex.

The rise and fall of Ceawlin is early proof that even the mightiest royal warlord was never completely secure in his kingship. The power of the Saxon kings was never absolute, nor could it be safeguarded by military strength. It depended on the fulfilment of an unwritten social contract between ruler and ruled. It was not enough for a king to be a respected leader of the host in war; he also had to 'be a good lord' to his subjects. This entailed constant demonstrations of justice, reliability, access-ibility, and speed to reward good and faithful service and punish wrongdoers. If, over the years, he showed that he lacked these qualities, the king and his heirs could be ousted and replaced by a new dynasty claiming kinship to the ancient ruling house.

The *Chronicle* entries for the late sixth century also provide the first reference to the king's lieutenants known as *ealdormen*: provincial viceroys in peace, commanders of the national army's regional divisions in war. It was natural that the most reliable members of the king's war council should become the permanent senior officials of his kingdom, and ealdormen feature prominently in the warfare and politics recorded by the *Chronicle*. The first two mentioned were Kentishmen, Oslaf and Cnebba, killed in battle at 'Wibbandun' in 568 when Ceawlin defeated Ethelbert.

The coming of Christianity in the late sixth and early seventh centuries gave the Saxon kings a new breed of counsellor – the bishops and abbots of the Church, whose evangelizing work was made possible only by royal consent. In return for kingly patronage the Church leaders offered advice, revenue and support which was both political and, on occasion, military. The wars of Saxon England produced a notable crop of fighting bishops who joined forces with the ealdormen in moments of military crisis.

Christianity was carried to the Anglo-Saxons on two opposing currents: from the Celtic Church founded at Iona in 565 by St Columba, originally of Ireland; and from the Roman mission headed by St Augustine, who landed in Kent about thirty-five years later (597). The supremacy of the Roman Church over the successors of Columba was finally accepted at the famous synod at Whitby in 664. It is significant that the Whitby conference was 'chaired' by King Oswiu of Northumbria, who cast the decisive vote in favour of Rome. The Northumbrian historian Bede finished his *History of the English Church and People* only sixty-seven years after Whitby, and if Bede is to be believed Oswiu silenced the wrangling ecclesiastics with a heartening blast of secular common sense. Having persuaded both parties to agree that Rome was the Church of St Peter, and that St Peter held the keys of heaven, Oswiu declared: 'Then, I tell you, Peter is guardian of the gates of heaven, and I shall not contradict him. I shall obey his commands in everything to the best of my knowledge and ability; otherwise,

OPPOSITE Prim Victorian depiction of Augustine preaching to Ethelbert of Kent, the mission which established the Roman Church in southern England. Royal patronage was essential for the conversion of the English, which later missionaries often found hard going.

20

Ford Madox Brown's mural of the baptism of Edwin of Northumbria by the missionary Paulinus.

when I come to the gates of heaven, there may be no one to open them ...'

Sheer persistence carried the Christian missionaries through in the end, but their progress was extremely erratic because no two kings reacted to the Christian message in the same way. Augustine's mission got off to a flying start because Ethelbert of Kent, recovering from his earlier humiliation by Ceawlin of Wessex, had made himself overlord of the whole of southern England by 597. Ethelbert had married a Christian Frankish princess, and was converted himself within a couple of years of Augustine's arrival. But when Ethelbert died in 616 his son and heir Eadbald reverted to paganism and it took until 640, when Eadbald died, before Kent became officially Christian again on the conversion of the new king, Eorcenberht. Ethelbert's

22

powerful ally, Raedwald of East Anglia, had accepted the Faith on approval, merely adding a Christian altar to one of his pagan temples to see if the new god really was better than the old. Edwin of Northumbria was similarly cautious in his acceptance of Christianity, which was certainly not the result of any eagerness to live a life of brotherly love. In 626 Edwin narrowly survived an assassination attempt by a West Saxon agent. Before setting off on the inevitable war of massacre and revenge at the expense of the West Saxons, Edwin gave Bishop Paulinus the chance to prove what Christian prayers for a Northumbrian victory could do. Impressed by the ease with which he exterminated his enemies, Edwin accepted conversion before the next year was out.

The fragile early links between Church and State in the Saxon kingdoms were greatly strengthened by the timely rise of a common enemy. For nearly twenty-five years – from about 632 to 655 – the Christian kings and their bishops found common cause in repeated wars against the most redoubtable symbol of paganism in arms. An implacable pagan to the day he died, the Mercian King Penda welded the Mercians and Middle Angles into a powerful central English kingdom and constantly harried his neighbours to the north and south. Penda defeated and killed two of the great Northumbrian kings of the seventh century, Edwin in 633 and Oswald in 641, before meeting his own death in battle at the hands of Oswald's brother Oswiu in 655. But even Bede, describing Penda's ruinous assaults on the Christian kingdoms, was scrupulous in pointing out the great redeeming feature of Penda's savage character: 'King Penda himself did not forbid the preaching of the Faith to any even of his own Mercians who wished to listen; but he hated and despised any whom he knew to be insincere in their practice of Christianity once they had accepted it, and said that any who despised the commandments of God in whom they professed to believe were themselves despicable wretches.'

Thus even Penda of Mercia, Saxon England's 'public enemy number one' in the seventh century, was honoured in later years for his probity as a lord. Penda's own son and heir, Peada, was baptized two years before Penda's death, and on Peada's accession in 655 the conversion of Mercia painlessly ensued.

The rise of Mercia completed the array of realms known as

OVERLEAF Seven columns for seven kingdoms: a visual 'supplement' to the *Chronicle* shows the leading monarchs of the heptarchy: (left to right) Kent and Essex, Wessex and Sussex, Mercia, East Anglia, Northumbria.

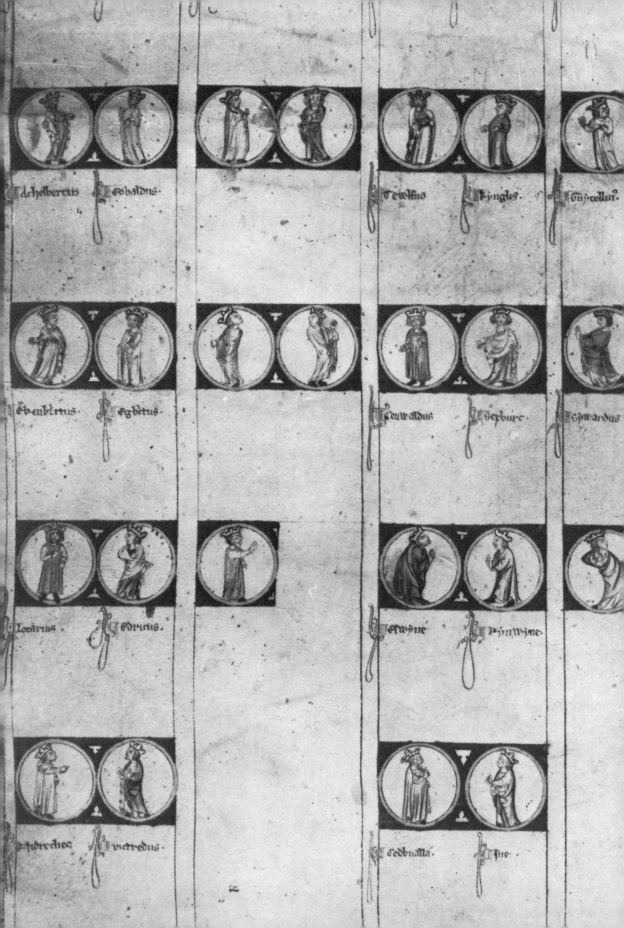

Adchelbertus   Cobaldus.   Tewlfus   Kynglus.   Conscellus

Ebenbertus   Egbertus.   Eduvaldus   Sepbure   Espuardus

Locarius   Cedricus.   Esluvine   Pinuvine.

Ædirechus   Uvictredus.   Cedbualla.   Jne.

Sebbyus. Wolfle. Penda. Sybertus. Egrydius. Oswaldus. Oswyn.

Sedelredus. Henda. Anna. Adelbertus. Egfridus. Alfridus.

Sedeltredus. Edelbaldus. Edwaldus. Walduffus. Ostredus. Eadbertus.

Kenredus. Coffa. Edmundus. Osulf. Ceoledelwardus.

the 'heptarchy', the seven kingdoms of Saxon England: Kent, Sussex, Wessex, Essex, Northumbria, East Anglia and Mercia. For the next 200 years, until the Danish armies shattered the old order of Saxon England for ever, there was a virtually unbroken succession of wars between the English kingdoms. Their rulers were rarely content with mere survival as a basic policy; where possible, they sought to eclipse and dominate their neighbours.

The kings who achieved this dominance were remembered as 'Bretwaldas', which meant 'rulers of Britain'. This grandiose title would be more accurately rendered as 'overlord of the

26

The splendour of Northumbrian art. This is the whalebone ivory Franks Casket from the early eighth century, when the temporal power of Northumbria was already on the wane.

English kingdoms'. It was not a hereditary title with a permanent imperial throne and regalia, but an honorific bestowed on an outstandingly successful and powerful king – a ruler who, in his lifetime, was able to demand anything from deference to instant obedience from the other English kings. Before the coming of the Danes in the middle of the ninth century, Essex was the only one of the seven kingdoms which failed to produce a Bretwalda. The *Chronicle* lists eight Bretwaldas, the first being Aelle of Sussex, the conqueror of Pevensey in 491. Then came Ceawlin of Wessex, Ethelbert of

imago leonis

O AGI
HAR
R

US
CUS

OPPOSITE Royal piety and patronage of the Church, the earliest expression of 'Church and State' in England. Here King Ecgfrith of Northumbria dedicates a new church to St Cuthbert.

LEFT St Mark, from the magnificent *Lindisfarne Gospels*, written and illustrated in about 700.

OVERLEAF The descent of the kings of Wessex, reconstructed from the *Anglo-Saxon Chronicle*.

Kent, and Ethelbert's former dependent, Raedwald of East Anglia. These were followed by the trio of seventh-century Northumbrian Bretwaldas, Edwin, Oswald and Oswiu, and finally by the West Saxon, Egbert, in the early ninth century.

However, the regional chauvinism of the *Chronicle* (compiled mainly in Northumbria and Wessex with a decided anti-Mercian bias) excludes the three great Mercian kings of the eighth century who certainly held the status of Bretwalda. These were Aethelbald (726–57), Offa (757–96) and Cenwulf (796–821). And it was in Offa's reign that the first prototype of

The old English ruling house
(line of Cerdic of Wessex)

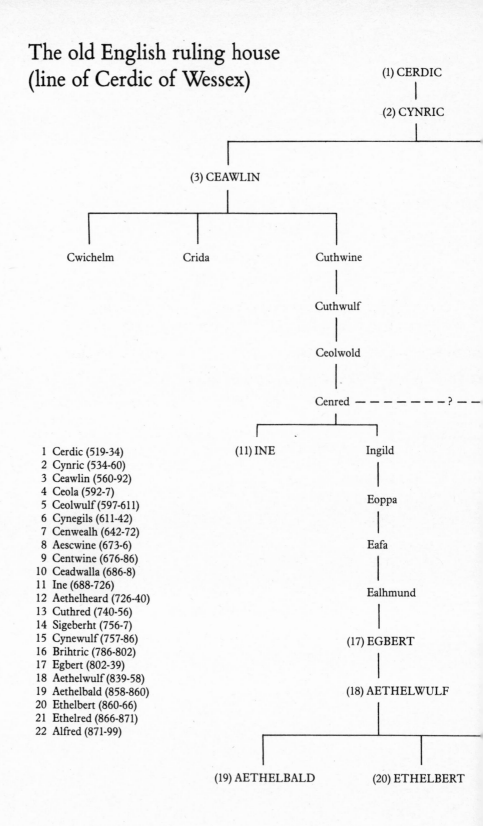

1 Cerdic (519-34)
2 Cynric (534-60)
3 Ceawlin (560-92)
4 Ceola (592-7)
5 Ceolwulf (597-611)
6 Cynegils (611-42)
7 Cenwealh (642-72)
8 Aescwine (673-6)
9 Centwine (676-86)
10 Ceadwalla (686-8)
11 Ine (688-726)
12 Aethelheard (726-40)
13 Cuthred (740-56)
14 Sigeberht (756-7)
15 Cynewulf (757-86)
16 Brihtric (786-802)
17 Egbert (802-39)
18 Aethelwulf (839-58)
19 Aethelbald (858-860)
20 Ethelbert (860-66)
21 Ethelred (866-871)
22 Alfred (871-99)

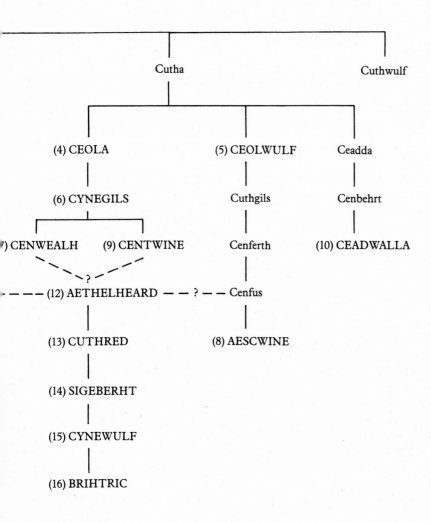

Cutha   Cuthwulf

(4) CEOLA   (5) CEOLWULF   Ceadda

(6) CYNEGILS   Cuthgils   Cenbehrt

⁊) CENWEALH   (9) CENTWINE   Cenferth   (10) CEADWALLA

?

‧ — — — (12) AETHELHEARD — — ? — — Cenfus

(13) CUTHRED   (8) AESCWINE

(14) SIGEBERHT

(15) CYNEWULF

(16) BRIHTRIC

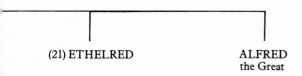

(21) ETHELRED   ALFRED
                           the Great

Saxon *England* – a nation subject to a single king of such authority that he could treat on equal terms with Charlemagne himself – came briefly into being.

The gorgeous contents of the Sutton Hoo ship burial, dating from the early seventh century and probably belonging to Raedwald of East Anglia, show that Bretwaldas before Offa had received rich gifts from the Continent. Bede states that Edwin of Northumbria had given himself quasi-imperial airs, being preceded by 'the standard known to the Romans as *Tufa*' wherever he walked or rode. Aethelbald of Mercia, Offa's predecessor, had formally claimed no more than the overlordship of southern England, to be 'king not only of the Mercians but of all the provinces known by the general name of southern English'. But Offa was the first on record to use the title of 'King of the English', and be treated as such by the arbiters of Europe.

It is tragic that Bede was born a century too early to write a detailed history of Offa and his reign. If such an account was ever written it has not survived, and all we have are tantalizing scraps of information, or a 'hollow shape', as Churchill has put it, 'in which a creature of unusual strength and size undoubtedly

32

resided'. Offa never sought to conquer the other six kingdoms and annex them to Mercia; his supremacy rested on intervention and exploitation, not the constant exercise of brute force. There was no need for military action against Northumbria. The northern kingdom wallowed in civil strife throughout Offa's reign, during which at least eight Northumbrian kings were made and unmade. Secure from the north (as his great-great-grand-uncle Penda had never been during the heyday of the seventh-century Northumbrian Bretwaldas), Offa was free to concentrate on dominating the south.

Several charters show Offa confirming enactments by the kings of Sussex, Kent and Wessex; in 794, we are bleakly told without further amplification, he had King Ethelbert of East Anglia beheaded. To maintain his supremacy in the south-east, Offa broke up an ominous dynastic merger between the ruling houses of Wessex and Kent, driving the king of Kent's son, Egbert, into exile in 786, and putting in his own candidate, Brihtric, to rule Wessex. Three years later, Brihtric's allegiance was cemented by his marriage to Offa's daughter, Eadburh.

The ninth-century 'Fuller Brooch' of silver, with the Five Senses of Man as the central theme.

For Offa this marriage, though politically useful, was a disappointing second-best: it came about only after the breakdown of negotiations with Offa's 'dearest brother' across the Channel: Charlemagne. Seeking a bride for his son Charles, the overlord of the Franks had asked for the daughter of the overlord of the English. Offa, however, seems to have stood on his dignity as the heir of a ruling house which had been producing kings long before Charlemagne's ancestors had ever been heard of. Charlemagne took exception to Offa's request that his daughter should marry Offa's son Ecgfrith, and closed his ports to English shipping. But diplomatic relations had been fully resumed by 796, the year of Offa's death, when Charlemagne sent Offa a fulsome letter announcing trade concessions to the benefit of English merchants. In this extraordinary letter, the master of Europe also asked Offa to restore the old measurements used for exports of English cloth.

Offa's enduring monument is the enormous dyke he had built to mark the frontier between the English and the Britons of Wales – a negotiated frontier, because Offa abandoned former English territory west of the dyke. He also successfully negotiated for a third English archbishopric (Lichfield) to be founded in Mercia, a political counterbalance to the archbishoprics of Canterbury in Kent and York in Northumbria. Not content with striking the most sophisticated coinage seen in Britain since the days of the Romans, Offa had his son Ecgfrith formally consecrated king in 787 – the first such ceremony in English history.

The essential point about Offa's supremacy as 'King of the English' is that it was a one-man political *tour de force*, a shrewd but temporary exploitation of the weaknesses of Mercia's rivals. Cenwulf, the new king (Offa's only son Ecgfrith died in the same year as his father, 796), managed to keep Egbert off the throne of Wessex only until 802. Five years later effective Mercian control of Kent ended with the death of King Cuthred, Cenwulf's brother. Egbert of Wessex not only completed the union of Kent and Wessex which Offa and Cenwulf had managed to postpone; he also went on to conquer Mercia itself in 829, ousting King Wiglaf, and receive the formal submission of Northumbria in the same year. But within a year Wiglaf was back on the throne of an independent Mercia.

Egbert was forced to accept the strong individual traditions of the other kingdoms, as Offa had done, and content himself with being the overlord of the south. When he died in 839 Egbert had achieved for Wessex what Aethelbald had achieved for Mercia and Edwin for Northumbria in the preceding two centuries: he had made his kingdom the leading 'superpower' in England. The loose but resilient network of the heptarchy made it impossible for him to do more.

Offa's Dyke, thrusting across Edenhope Hill near Mainstone in Shropshire.

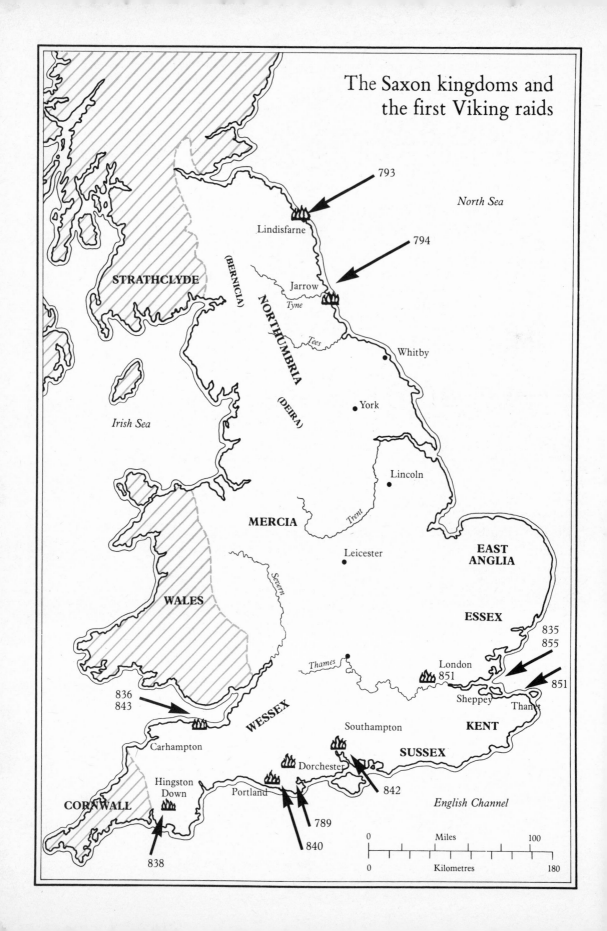

The Saxon kingdoms and the first Viking raids

North Sea

793

794

Lindisfarne

Jarrow

Tyne

Tees

Whitby

STRATHCLYDE

(BERNICIA)

NORTHUMBRIA

(DEIRA)

York

Irish Sea

Lincoln

Trent

MERCIA

EAST ANGLIA

Leicester

ESSEX

835
855

WALES

Severn

Thames

London
851

851

Sheppey

Thanet

836
843

WESSEX

KENT

Southampton

Carhampton

Dorchester

SUSSEX

Hingston Down

Portland

842

CORNWALL

789

English Channel

838

840

| 0 | | | | | Miles | | | | 100 |
| 0 | | | | | Kilometres | | | | 180 |

What would have happened to Saxon England if that network had not been destroyed by the Danish invasions later in the ninth century, allowing Wessex to emerge as *the* kingdom of England? Almost certainly there would have been more Bretwaldas to re-create the power enjoyed by Offa. Perhaps a precarious, federated English kingdom would have evolved naturally, although this would have entailed so much surrender of power by the subject kingdoms that it is impossible to guess how long the process would have taken. In any event, the English were denied any choice in the matter. Within a century of Offa's death, the Danish invaders had annihilated the old order of the English kingdoms with the brutal formula, 'Four minus three leaves one'.

ABOVE Vivid image of Viking terror on a gravestone at Lindisfarne: a force of 'heathen men' on the rampage.

OPPOSITE Saxon England in the last years of the heptarchy, showing the first Viking raids.

2 Alfred 'the Great'

871-899

DESPITE HIS UNDOUBTED POWER and claims to be 'King of the English', even Offa of Mercia had never acquired the unquestioned status which would have made his authority permanent and hereditary. This was the status of national *leader* of all Englishmen, whether Northumbrian, Mercian, East Anglian, Kentishman or West Saxon. The subject's awareness of the king as national leader is the vital spark that makes monarchy a real and living phenomenon; and Alfred of Wessex was the first of the Saxon kings to kindle that spark outside his own kingdom. He did it by showing that the terrifying Danes could be fought and beaten; and by the time he had achieved this, his prowess could not be imitated by other English kings. No other English kings had survived. Alfred of Wessex (born in 849) stood alone, as the *Chronicle* puts it, 'King over the whole English people except for that part which was under Danish rule'.

The first recorded attacks on Saxon England by Viking freebooters from Scandinavia (not *all* of them can have been 'Danes', as the *Chronicle* and other English sources imply) came at the end of the eighth century. In 789 'three ships of Northmen' landed in Weymouth Bay. They do not seem to have accomplished much; after killing the official who tried to take them to King Brihtric of Wessex at Dorchester, they re-embarked. However, in 793 and 794, two successive raids hit the famous monasteries of Lindisfarne and Jarrow in Northumbria, showing that the favourite targets for the early raiders were the rich churches and monasteries studding the land. Here was loot in abundance: not only Church plate but slaves in the form of monastic novices.

If their ships were of the same dimensions as the Viking Gokstad ship, 'three ships of Northmen' could have landed a raiding force consisting of about 100 warriors. Almost certainly there were more early raids than those recorded in the *Chronicle* and other histories; it is hard to believe that there really was a forty-year respite between the raid on Jarrow in 794 and the ravaging of the Isle of Sheppey in 835. But from 835 a mounting tempo of attacks got under way with increasingly large Viking fleets. By 852 the first raiding force had dug in and spent a winter on English soil (on the Isle of Thanet in Kent). From then on the attacks intensified until the 'Great Army' of the Danes landed in 866, bent on conquest rather than mere plunder.

The English kingdoms stood up well to the early attacks. Forces raised by the local ealdormen (or the king himself, if he happened to be in the area) seem to have stood an equal chance of defeating the raiders in battle. In 840, for example:

> Ealdorman Wulfheard fought at Southampton against the crews of 33 ships, and made a great slaughter there and had the victory; and Wulfheard died that year. And the same year Ealdorman Aethelhelm with the people of Dorset fought against the Danish army at Portland, and for a long time he put the enemy to flight; and the Danes had possession of the battlefield and killed the ealdorman.

These were the third and fourth Viking attacks since the ravaging of Sheppey in 835. Egbert of Wessex was badly beaten at Carhampton in 836, fighting the crews of thirty-five ships; the following year, however, Egbert smashed a second attack in the West Country at Hingston Down. The main trouble was the proliferation of Viking bases – in the Hebrides, the Isle of Man and Ireland, as well as Scandinavia itself – which enabled them to strike where they chose on the long English coastline. But on the whole the 'heathen men' remained a pest that could be coped with, even after they learned to support themselves on English soil. Until the coming of the Great Army in 866 the English gave as good as they got. When Alfred of Wessex was born at Wantage in 849 the biggest problem facing the kingdom was not the 'heathen men'; it was the worrying style of kingship practised by Alfred's father, King Aethelwulf.

Aethelwulf had succeeded his father Egbert in 839. Egbert was a grizzled veteran who had fought for survival from his youth; Aethelwulf came naturally to the throne of Wessex. He proved to be an intensely religious man, cursed with little political sense and too many able and ambitious sons. His first act was to split the swollen kingdom created by Egbert, giving the eastern half (Kent, Essex, Surrey and Sussex) to his eldest son Athelstan and keeping the ancient western heartland of Wessex (Hampshire, Wiltshire, Dorset and Devon) for himself. As the youngest atheling or 'prince of the blood', the young Alfred had no prospects of ruling. He had four elder brothers to precede him: Athelstan, Aethelbald, Ethelbert and Ethelred.

ABOVE The mitre-shaped gold and niello ring of Aethelwulf, Alfred's father.

PREVIOUS PAGES 'Alfred submitting his laws to the Witan', by John Bridges. The king is shown with his queen, Elswitha, and eldest son Edward.

41

According to Alfred's biographer, Asser, Alfred's mother Osburh was descended from Stuf and Wihtgar, ancestral conquerors of the Isle of Wight. Though 'a very religious woman, noble in character, noble also by birth', Osburh also seems to have been an utterly human mother who lavished attention on her youngest son. The earliest of the many stories about Alfred is that Osburh encouraged him to read and write, offering a beautifully illuminated book to the first of her sons who could read it to her. His fancy taken by the beauty of the book's initial letter, Alfred took the book to his tutor and asked him to read it. He then used his remarkable memory to outpace his brothers, claiming the prize by reciting the whole book to Osburh without a fault.

Alfred stands out as an unusually bright boy who suffered from indifferent teaching, for he later told Asser that he had always resented not having been taught to read and write properly until he was in his teens. Certainly he was no cloistered bookworm, nor was he dominated by religious devotion. Though he would listen to Saxon poems by the hour, committing them to memory, he also loved the strenuous exercise provided by all forms of hunting. From an early age he showed himself perfectly confident in the world of men, poised without being unpleasantly precocious. Alfred was only five when King Aethelwulf sent him to the court of Pope Leo IV in Rome. Alfred came home from this state visit with the insignia and dignity of a Roman Consul which Leo had conferred on him.

Alfred's visit to Rome in 853 certainly shows that Saxon England was still taking the Viking menace in its stride. Aethelwulf would probably have gone to Rome himself, but he was campaigning against the Welsh with King Burgred of Mercia. The King would perhaps have served his people better if he had stayed in the south. While Aethelwulf and Burgred were winning cheap victories in Wales, 'Ealhhere with the people of Kent and Huda with the people of Surrey fought in Thanet against the heathen army, and at first had the victory; and many men on both sides were killed and drowned there, and both the Ealdormen killed.' A major mystery of this period is the fate of Athelstan, the son whom Aethelwulf had installed as king of the south-east. He is last mentioned in the *Chronicle*

entry for 851, fighting a spirited campaign of his own: 'King Athelstan and Ealdorman Ealhhere fought in ships and slew a great army at Sandwich in Kent, and captured nine ships and put the others to flight.' So runs the laconic reference to the earliest recorded naval victory in English history. Though no date is given for Athelstan's death, he had vanished from the scene by the time of the Thanet campaign of 853.

Two years later King Aethelwulf himself set out for Rome, taking Alfred with him. The King seems to have been

Viking longship under sail, from Gotland in Sweden.

43

extraordinarily detached from the anxieties of his people in the south-east, for 855 was the year in which Viking raiders wintered on the Isle of Sheppey for the first time. Aethelwulf and Alfred spent a year in Rome before returning home via the court of Charles the Bald, king of the West Franks: the first recorded state visit of an English king to a Continental court. For Alfred these experiences (completely untypical for a six-year-old Saxon atheling) must have been particularly memorable because they included the acquisition of a stepmother. Aethelwulf's new bride was Judith, daughter of Charles the Bald. (We do not know when Osburh died, but if the story about Alfred and the illuminated book is true she must have lived until about 853–4; if the year of her death was much earlier, she would have found herself presenting the book to a toddler of truly miraculous gifts.)

Late in 856 Aethelwulf and Alfred came home to acute crisis. Aethelbald, eldest of the athelings since Athelstan's death, had hatched a conspiracy with the Ealdorman of Somerset and the Bishop of Sherborne to oppose Aethelwulf's resumption of the kingship when he returned. There was, apparently, more than enough loyal support for Aethelwulf to start a first-class civil war if he chose, or even to have made certain of the banishment of Aethelbald and his fellow conspirators. But the King chose neither alternative. Instead he yielded Wessex proper to his upstart son and accepted Kent, Sussex, Surrey and Essex for himself, ruling there until his death in 858.

Aethelwulf's restoration included a special concession which throws an interesting light on the role of the Saxon queens. This had always tended to be passive, and the exceptions proved the rule. The pagan Bretwalda, Ethelbert of Kent, had allowed his Frankish Queen, Bertha, to practise Christianity before the arrival of Augustine's mission in 597. When Cenwealh of Wessex died in 672, his widow, Queen Seaxburh, reigned for a year after him. In 697, according to one of the *Chronicle's* most cryptic entries, Osthryth, sister of King Ecgfrith of Northumbria and the Queen of Ethelred of Mercia, was killed 'by the Southumbrians' (presumably her disaffected Mercian subjects). But in Wessex the evil behaviour of Eadburh, the daughter of Offa of Mercia who married King Brihtric, caused a severe reaction against consorts with excessive status. Asser states that

44

after Eadburh 'the West Saxons did not allow the queen to sit next the king, or even be called queen, but "wife of the king"'. This restriction was lifted for Queen Judith, high-ranking European princess that she was, for the brief remainder of her husband's life. The episode is another example of how court protocol in Saxon England was still being moulded by influences from across the Channel in the last years of the heptarchy.

The position of Judith remained a special one as long as Aethelwulf lived; after his death in 858 it became notorious, for Aethelbald, the new king, outraged convention by marrying his father's widow. Asser piously laments the fact that this was 'contrary to God's prohibition and Christian dignity, and also against the usage of all pagans'; but the fact remains that the West Saxons accepted the rule of a man who was not only guilty of conspiracy against his own father but of incest as well. Aethelbald was able to make good his claim to the throne because he was next in the line of succession, and the black marks on his character were not enough to prevent him from becoming king. Nor do his brothers Ethelbert and Ethelred (Alfred was still only nine) seem to have made any notable challenge to Aethelbald's fitness to rule. In this the younger athelings may have been moved to respect their father's example in 856, which had been a model of Christian forbearance if not of political acumen. Aethelwulf's own will, which restricted Aethelbald's claim to rule to Wessex only, excluding the south-east, was certainly observed, with Ethelbert becoming king of the south-east. But the accession of Aethelbald shows that the West Saxons had come a long way from their ancient traditions, when the new king was elected by the councillors of the realm – the ealdormen and, after the coming of Christianity, the bishops. The old ritual was still observed and merit still mattered, as the accessions of Alfred and his son Edward were to prove; but by the end of the ninth century the election of a new king was becoming virtually automatic in Wessex.

The biggest problem in 858 was Aethelbald's readiness to flout convention and bend the rules, which proved that he was an unsafe lord to follow. There was general relief when he died in 860 after a reign of only two years, and harmony was restored by the accession of Ethelbert 'to the whole kingdom' – Wessex and the south-east combined. Restoring the united kingdom created by the great Egbert was an obvious, sensible way of clearing up the confusion caused by Aethelwulf's attempts to share out his patrimony, but it also created a highly important precedent. This was the political technique, used by later new kings anxious to restore order after a period of domestic disorder, of deliberately evoking memories of the last efficient king to rule. Canute was to do it when he became king of the English in 1016, ignoring the chaotic reign of Ethelred and harking back to the golden years of Edgar. Even William of Normandy followed suit after Hastings, ignoring Harold's usurpation and assuring his new subjects that he proposed to rule 'as in the time of King Edward'.

Ethelbert's reign (860–5) contained two further lessons for Alfred, who now ranked second in line of succession to the throne. Some time between 860 and 864 a powerful Viking army stormed north from Southampton Water and sacked the West Saxon capital itself: Winchester. This traumatic event was swiftly avenged by the ealdormen of Hampshire and Berkshire, who joined forces and shattered the raiders as they headed back to their ships laden with booty. Here was convincing proof of the West Saxons' resilient defence system and the efficacy of timely military action, but it was followed in 865 by a demonstration of a different kind, showing the uselessness of appeasement. A raiding force dug in on the Isle of Thanet and opened negotiations with the people of Kent, who agreed to pay a cash ransom in exchange for peace (the first recorded instance of the protection-money known in later years as 'Danegeld'). Having lulled the Kentishmen into a false sense of security, the raiders then stole across to the mainland and ravaged the east of the kingdom; 'for they knew', as Asser comments, 'that they would seize more money by secret plunder than by peace.'

As Ethelbert had produced no heir, when he died in 865 the kingdom passed to his eldest surviving brother, Ethelred; and with Ethelred's accession in 866, Saxon England's fight for survival began in earnest. For 866 was the year in which the Great Army of the Danes landed in East Anglia and set about the destruction of every kingdom in the island.

OPPOSITE The Great Army's assault on Saxon England in 866, with subsequent lines of march and Guthrum's invasion of Wessex ten years later.

46

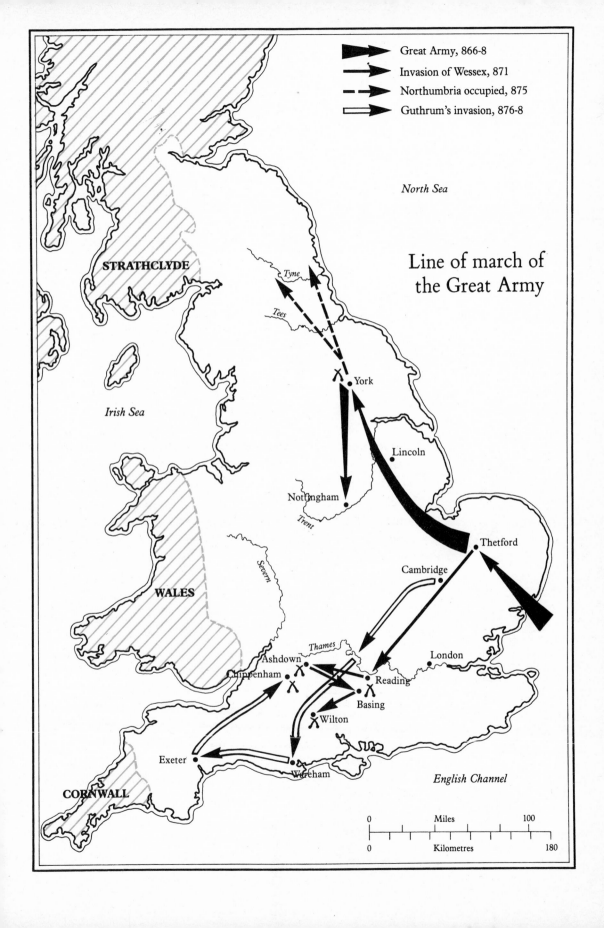

Line of march of the Great Army

Great Army, 866-8
Invasion of Wessex, 871
Northumbria occupied, 875
Guthrum's invasion, 876-8

North Sea

STRATHCLYDE

Tyne

Tees

Irish Sea

York

Lincoln

Nottingham

Trent

Thetford

Cambridge

Severn

WALES

Thames

Ashdown

Chippenham

London

Reading

Basing

Wilton

Exeter

Wareham

English Channel

CORNWALL

| 0 | Miles | 100 |
| 0 | Kilometres | 180 |

The English were used to raids and plundering armies, but they had never faced an enemy like this. It was said that the Great Army was led by the vengeful sons of the legendary Viking Ragnar Lothbrok, 'Hairy-breeches', who had been captured and ingloriously slain by the Northumbrians. From the outset of its career of terror in England, the Great Army behaved as no other Viking raiders had done. Descending on East Anglia in 866, they made a rapid peace with King Edmund of the East Angles and proceeded to round up every horse that could be found. Then, in 867, the Army rode *en masse* north across the Humber to invade Northumbria, which was, as usual, weltering in the throes of civil war. The Danish host ensconced itself inside the old Roman walls of York and shattered the belated attempts of the warring Northumbrians to join forces against the common enemy. 'An immense slaughter was made of the Northumbrians,' records the *Chronicle*, 'and both [Northumbrian] kings were killed, and the survivors made peace with the enemy.'

Over the next seven years, the Great Army demonstrated the fatal inability of the Saxon kingdoms to achieve a common defence policy with prompt and effective mutual aid. In 868, leaving prostrate Northumbria under a puppet-king, Egbert, the Army swept south into Mercia and seized Nottingham as its base for the year. King Burgred of Mercia had married a daughter of Aethelwulf in 853, and he now appealed to his brother-in-law Ethelred of Wessex for aid. Accompanied by Alfred, nineteen years old and exercising high command for the first time, Ethelred went north with a West Saxon army. The Mercians and West Saxons blockaded the Army inside Nottingham, but this promising start was wasted. Refusing either to attack the Army in its defences or starve it out, Burgred decided on a negotiated peace which left the Danish force completely intact. The squandering of this priceless opportunity certainly did not go unnoticed as Alfred and Ethelred led the West Saxons home; the Army returned undefeated and undamaged to York, and stayed there for the whole of 869.

Having tamely yielded the initiative to the enemy, Saxon England paid the inevitable penalty in 870. The Great Army flung itself on East Anglia, wiped out its armed forces and tortured King Edmund to death. Of the heptarchy's original

seven kingdoms Kent, Sussex and Essex had been absorbed by Wessex; Northumbria and East Anglia now lay under Danish occupation; only Mercia and Wessex were left. The leaders of the Great Army now turned on Wessex, whose forces had helped trap the Army in Mercia two years before.

In the amazing year of 871, Ethelred and Alfred gave the Great Army opposition such as it had never known since its arrival in England. There were five pitched battles before Easter with first blood going to the Berkshiremen, who ambushed a Danish force at Englefield and killed one of its commanding earls. Cheered by this victory, Ethelred and Alfred led the main army of Wessex against the Danish base at Reading, only to be repulsed with the loss of Ealdorman Aethelwulf, the victor of Englefield. The Great Army followed the West Saxon host as the latter withdrew westwards, but only four days after the defeat at Reading the West Saxons counter-attacked at Ashdown.

This was always remembered as Alfred's battle. He led his

The martyrdom of Edmund, last king of East Anglia, depicted in stained glass at Greensted Church, Essex.

49

troops 'like a wild boar' against the division commanded by the Danish earls, while Ethelred was still completing his eve-of-battle devotions in his tent. Five Danish earls were killed, while Ethelred's assault on the division commanded by the two kings, Healfdene and Bagsecg, resulted in the latter's death and the retreat of the Army. But the West Saxon victory at Ashdown did not end the campaign. The Army re-formed, and over the following weeks manoeuvred their opponents deeper and deeper into Wessex. In two more hard-fought battles – at Basing and a place called Meretun – the Danes ended the day in possession of the battlefield. What was worse, after the Meretun fight the Great Army received powerful reinforcements up the Thames. And then King Ethelred died, shortly after Easter. His son Aethelwold was still a baby, and Alfred, last of the sons of Aethelwulf, was the inevitable choice as successor of the war council of Wessex.

While Ethelred was still alive, he and Alfred seem to have agreed that the only sensible policy, with regard to the Great Army, was to fight and fight again until the Army decided to seek easier prey elsewhere. Alfred's first decision as king was to keep the army of Wessex in the field. Only a month after his election as king he was badly beaten by the Army at Wilton, but still he refused to give up. 'And during that year', states the *Chronicle* proudly, 'nine general engagements were fought against the Danish army in the kingdom south of the Thames, besides the expeditions which [Alfred] and ealdormen and king's thanes often rode on, which were not counted. And that year nine [Danish] earls were killed and one king. And the West Saxons made peace with the enemy that year.'

Although the wording of that last sentence shows that it was Alfred who asked for the armistice, it is equally clear that, after the tremendous campaign of 871, the Great Army had had quite enough of Wessex for the immediate future. In 872 the Danes moved their base east from Reading to the Mercian town of London. Events in that year made the truce with Wessex doubly welcome to the Army, for the Northumbrians revolted. They drove out Egbert, their quisling king, and the Archbishop of York, both of whom were granted asylum by Burgred of Mercia. It was Burgred's last act of appeasement towards the Danes. After crushing the Northumbrians for the second time in 873, the Army descended on Mercia in the following year

... and drove King Burgred across the sea, after he had held the kingdom 22 years. And they conquered all that land. And he went to Rome and settled there; and his body is buried in the church of St Mary in the English quarter. And the same year they gave the kingdom of the Mercians to be held by Ceolwulf, a foolish king's thane; and he swore oaths to them and gave hostages, that it should be ready for them on whatever day they wished to have it, and he would be ready, himself and all who would follow him, at the enemy's service. (*Anglo-Saxon Chronicle*)

Wessex was now completely isolated, but the inevitable showdown with the last of the independent Saxon kingdoms was delayed by significant events on the Danish side. In 875, for the first time since its arrival in England nine years before, the Great Army began to split up. Healfdene led his division north to begin the settlement of Northumbria; Guthrum, Oscetel and Anwend headed for Cambridge 'with a great force', and remained there throughout 875. This must have been cheering news for Alfred and the West Saxons – knowing that from 875 they would no longer be confronted by *the* Army, but only by part of it.

In the four years' respite since the 871 campaign, Alfred had imitated his dead brother Athelstan and formed a small naval force, in order to give the maximum trouble to the invaders by sea as well as on land. He led this force to sea in 875 and attacked a small Viking fleet of seven ships, capturing one and putting the others to flight. It was an encouraging start; but he was totally surprised by the energy and cunning which Guthrum displayed in the land assault on Wessex which began in 876.

The invasion started with Guthrum's army racing south-west from Cambridge, slipping clean past the incomplete muster of Wessex, and digging in at Wareham in Dorset. When Alfred caught up with Guthrum's army it was in too strong a position to be attacked, and Alfred again resorted to negotiation. Guthrum now proved himself a master of deceit, offering hostages and the most binding oaths to evacuate Wessex; then, with the talks still under way, breaking out by night and speeding further west to dig in again at Exeter in early 877. Then Guthrum's own plan went badly awry. His adherence to the line of the south coast had enabled a powerful Danish fleet to

Guthrum enthroned,
from a fourteenth-century
Icelandic manuscript.

keep pace with the army of Cambridge – but as the fleet passed Swanage on its way to Exeter it was scattered by a great storm, and 120 ships were lost.

Temporary stalemate was accepted in the West; Alfred's army was still too small to attack Guthrum's, which remained dangerously isolated, but it was Guthrum who got the best of the ensuing negotiations. He already knew that the English could not keep an army in the field the whole year round, and

52

that the biggest weakness in Alfred's army during a long campaign was the accelerating wastage of manpower as soldiers went home to attend to the harvest. Guthrum therefore timed his negotiations for completion *before* the 877 harvest, agreeing to evacuate Wessex at once. These were terms which Alfred could not refuse – but they also ensured the dispersal of the West Saxon army until the spring of 878.

Guthrum then bided his time before unleashing his master-stroke: an assault in the middle of winter, which no Danish force had ever attempted before and for which Wessex was wholly unprepared. In January 878 Guthrum's army, believed to be snugly wintering in Mercia, hurled itself on Alfred's royal residence at Chippenham and drove Alfred, his wife Elswitha and his young children headlong into exile to avoid capture. With great prescience, the Danish king then seems to have treated the prostrate West Saxons as his natural subjects instead of his victims, arguing that Alfred had deserted his people as Burgred had deserted the Mercians four years before. 'And the people submitted to [the Danes]', admits the *Chronicle*, 'except King Alfred. He journeyed in difficulties through the woods and fen-fastnesses with a small force.'

Alfred's 'finest hour' had come: the late winter and spring of 878, which he spent as a fugitive on the Isle of Athelney, still refusing to give up although most of his subjects accepted that his cause was lost. From these weeks of utter humiliation sprang the story of Alfred allowing the old woman's bread to burn as he sat lost in thought, then patiently enduring her torrent of abuse. However, by no means all of Wessex had submitted to the Danes, and this was largely due to the example which Alfred himself had set. While he lay in hiding on Athelney, laboriously spreading the news that he was still alive and in the kingdom, the men of Devon fought on without him. They smashed a raiding fleet of twenty-three ships, killed its commander – one of the dreaded Ragnarsson brothers – and wiped out the army it landed. Most important of all, the Devon men captured the Danes' most prized military totem: the 'Raven' banner, which was said to flutter its wings before a victory and hang limp before a defeat. This victory in Devon, not won by Alfred in person but arguably inspired by him, was the first positive stirring of the victorious recoil of Wessex in 878.

The 'Alfred Jewel' of gold and enamel, inscribed 'Alfred had me made'. Found near the king's refuge at Athelney, it inspired G.K. Chesterton in his splendid *Ballad of the White Horse:*

> One dim ancestral jewel hung
> On his ruined armour grey;
> He rent and cast it at her feet:
> Where, after centuries, with slow feet,
> Men came from hall and school and street
> And found it where it lay.

By Easter 878 Alfred had already converted Athelney into a fortified base for guerrilla attacks on the nearest Danish outposts, and the news that the king was still alive and fighting was spreading fast. Seven weeks after Easter, Alfred was ready to take the field. He concentrated the musters of Somerset, Wiltshire and west Hampshire and advanced rapidly to attack Guthrum's army at Edington, on the northern edge of Salisbury Plain. Of Edington, the most momentous battle of Alfred's reign, the *Chronicle* says simply that he 'fought against the whole army and put it to flight'. What mattered was the astonishing aftermath. Guthrum abandoned all the trickery which had confounded Alfred in the previous year; he accepted Christian baptism, swore to leave Wessex, and this time was as good as his word. Guthrum eventually led his army into East Anglia, settling there in 880 and remaining a trustworthy neighbour to Wessex until his death ten years later.

If Alfred had died the year after Edington, his dogged preservation of Wessex against all odds would have been enough to earn him a secure niche in history. But he was to reign for another twenty years, and in 879, his thirtieth year, his greatest achievements still lay before him.

The first of these was improved security for the people of Wessex, using a simple system which could be adopted by communities of free Englishmen anywhere in the island. Alfred's overhaul of the defences of Wessex was naturally dictated by the problems he had encountered. The traditional call-up in times of emergency – the *fyrd* – could cope with raids by isolated Viking fleets; but it was inadequate for raising a national army to resist a menace like the Great Army of 866–75, or even Guthrum's army of 876–8. Wessex needed a national army that would not melt away as harvest-time approached, or when the regional contingents decided that they were being asked to campaign too far away from home. Alfred judged, correctly, that there was every chance of Wessex being attacked by another Danish army in the future, and that the West Saxons might have to stay on campaign for months, marching if necessary from Kent to Devon and back to keep up the pressure on the enemy. He therefore introduced a rota system into the fyrd by which half the men of fighting age reported for duty when summoned by their ealdormen, and the other half stayed at home. If the ensuing campaign turned out to be a long one, the first contingents to take the field could be relieved by fresh troops without total disruption to the domestic farming year.

Apart from this reform of the fyrd, Alfred planned a national system of local defence. He saw no reason why, if the Danes could protect their armies in the field by digging and building fortifications, his subjects should not do the same. A raiding force or invading army thrived by terrorizing and living off the country; it arrived, dug in, then either held the surrounding region up to ransom, looted it bare, or did both before moving on to pastures new. After 878 Alfred planned to counter this by the building of carefully sited *burhs* – fortified areas, surrounded by ditch and wall, into which the local countrymen or townsmen could take their families, goods and livestock when menaced by invaders. The new network of burhs was far from complete when Alfred died, but it had already radically changed the prospects for invaders. These now tended to encounter a scoured countryside and a defiant garrison which could hold out until the main field army advanced to its rescue.

The new defence arrangements paid rapid dividends. In 855 the powerful army which had been savaging the kingdom of the West Franks for the past four years split. One wing of this army crossed the Channel, swept up the Medway and attacked Rochester

... where they besieged the city and made other fortifications around themselves. And nevertheless the English defended the city until King Alfred came up with his army. Then the enemy went to their ships and abandoned their fortification, and they were deprived of their horses there, and immediately that same summer they went back across the sea.

Alfred's fleet defeating the Danes at sea, by Colin Gill.

Note that the *Chronicle*, describing this significant episode, says that the victory was won by 'the English' – not the men of Kent, or citizens of Rochester, or even the West Saxons. Already, it can be said, a new awareness of national identity was creeping in. This is confirmed by Alfred's reaction to sporadic trouble from the Danes in East Anglia in 885, which highlighted the danger posed by the open road of the lower Thames. In 885 Alfred attacked and took London, converting it into a burh. It was the first expansionist move made by Wessex since Egbert's time, half a century before, but the *Chronicle* does not describe it as just another West Saxon conquest. After Alfred took London, we are told, 'all the English people that were not under subjugation to the Danes submitted to him'.

Alfred was now king of the English in all but name – and that name he never took for himself. He regarded himself as no more than King of Wessex, and a caretaker king at that; he would never have become king at all if his brothers had not died early, and his immediate predecessor Ethelred had left an heir, the atheling Aethelwold, who would have as good a claim or better than Alfred's own son Edward when Alfred died. For the moment, Alfred knew that it was up to him to salvage all that was best and enduring from the wreckage created by the Danish onslaughts. He had no intention of jeopardizing the new stirrings of English unity by marching roughshod over regional tradition, or of proclaiming a strange new era in England. Acutely aware that London was Mercian property by tradition, he turned London over to the man who had assumed command over all free Mercians not content to live under Danish occupation: Ealdorman Ethelred. Alfred also revived the family tie with the Mercians, which dated from his father's reign. His own wife Elswitha, whom he married while still an atheling during Ethelred's reign, was the daughter of a Mercian ealdorman; and as soon as his eldest daughter Aethelflaed reached marriageable age, Alfred gave her to Ethelred of Mercia. In Ethelred, Alfred had a powerful ally north of the Thames – independent in theory, a willing viceroy in practice.

Ethelred of Mercia was not the only non-West Saxon whose voice was heard at Alfred's court, which after 886 was the focus for every leading Englishman, lay and secular. This made Alfred the first king of Wessex to have an array of English

ÆLFred kyning hateð gretan wærferð biscep his wordum luflice ⁊ freondlice; ⁊ ðe cyðan hate ðæt me com swiðe oft on gemynd, hwelce wiotan iu wæron giond Angelcynn, ægðer ge godcundra hada ge woruldcundra; ⁊ hu gesæliglica tida ða wæron giond Angelcynn; ⁊ hu ða kyningas ðe ðone onwald hæfdon ðæs folces on ðam dagum Gode ⁊ his ærendwrecum hyrsumedon; ⁊ hie ægðer ge hiora sibbe ge hiora siodo ge hiora onweald innanbordes gehioldon, ⁊ eac ut hiora eðel gerymdon; ⁊ hu him ða speow ægðer ge mid wige ge mid wisdome...

councillors. They advised Alfred when he drew up the treaty with Guthrum of East Anglia after the capture of London in 886: '... the peace which King Alfred and King Guthrum and the councillors of all the English race and all the people which is in East Anglia have all agreed on and confirmed with oaths'. The purpose of the treaty was to define a frontier between Guthrum's kingdom and unoccupied England; but it went far beyond that. The treaty agreed to 'estimate Englishman and

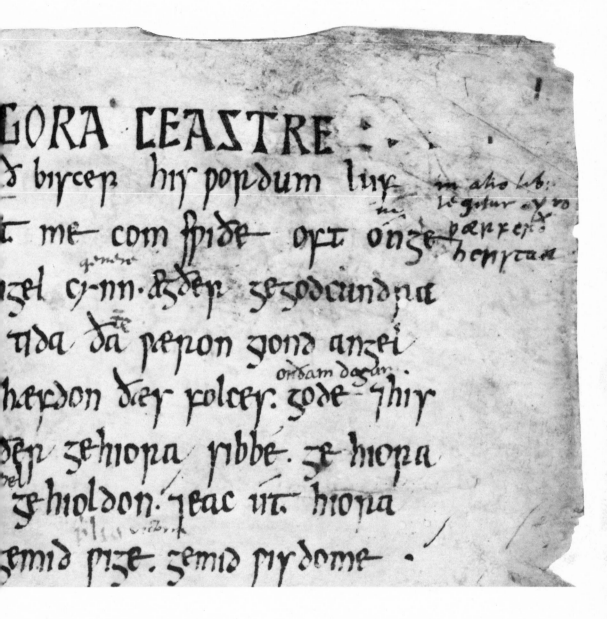

Facsimile of Alfred's translation into English of Pope Gregory's *Pastoral Care*.

Dane at the same amount' in law, and to facilitate trade exchanges between the two kingdoms. In short, Englishmen living under Danish occupation were not to be regarded as second-class citizens, and Danes occupying English soil were to be regarded as folk with whom free Englishmen could do business on equal terms. The implications for future relations between Englishmen and Danes were tremendous. Alfred's treaty with Guthrum is the first known English state document to have been drawn up to meet the interests of 'all the English race'; and its immense value as a precedent entitles it to rank with Magna Carta as one of the most formative documents in English history.

An equally enduring landmark was the new code of English law which Alfred compiled. This was notably conservative, drawing heavily on law codes issued by earlier kings of the heptarchy. Alfred took pains to spell this out in his preamble to the code, which does much to illustrate his policies and his basic approach to the duties of kingship. He wrote of earlier kings and their laws, and how they

> ... in many synods fixed the compensations for many human misdeeds, and they wrote them in many synod-books, here one law, there another.
>
> Then I, King Alfred, collected these together and ordered to be written many of them which our forefathers observed, those which I liked; and many of those which I did not like, I rejected with the advice of my councillors, and ordered them to be differently observed. For I dared not presume to set in writing at all many of my own, because it was unknown to me what would please those who should come after us. But those which I found anywhere, which seemed to me most just, either of the time of my kinsman, King Ine, or of Offa, king of the Mercians, or of Ethelbert, who first among the English received baptism, I collected herein, and omitted the others.
>
> Then I, Alfred, king of the West Saxons, showed these to all my councillors, and they then said that they were pleased to observe them.

Alfred's law code therefore explicitly avoided embarking on new legal provisions which later generations might find untenable. It was the first law code drawn up to meet the needs of Englishmen from all parts of the country – Wessex, Kent, Mercia and Northumbria – and, as such, it was the starting-point for all legislating kings of England who followed Alfred. The vital role of the king as law-giver was one of the most important traditions which Alfred kept alive and passed on to his successors.

Hardly less important was the tradition of the king as patron of the Church, of learning and the arts, for which Alfred was naturally remembered with special affection by ecclesiastical

OPPOSITE Alfred's statue at Winchester.

writers like Asser. The energetic restoration of the English Church and especially the monastic communities, which had been favourite targets for heathen plunderers since the first Viking raids a century before, made possible the great blossoming of English culture and learning in the tenth century. It is unlikely that any king other than Alfred would have given such a high priority to this aspect of national reconstruction. His two visits to Rome in boyhood had of course left him with a particular veneration for the Church and its role as the fount of all learning; but it took a very special king, in the early Middle Ages, to turn scholar himself and translate key texts for the benefit of his people. And not a single king or queen of England since Alfred has ever attempted to do the same.

In the last seven years of his life Alfred translated five works from Latin into English. These were Pope Gregory's *Pastoral Care* (a handbook for the clergy), Orosius' *History* of the ancient world (including Alfred's own observations on the origins of the English peoples), Bede's *Ecclesiastical History*, Boethius' *On the Consolation of Philosophy*, and St Augustine's *Soliloquies*. This feat is all the more impressive because it was between 892 and 896 that a second plundering army landed in England. Alfred's new defences held out, but they were kept at full stretch for four years. So, far from contenting himself with the role of soldier-king, ending his days embittered, brutalized and cynical (and who could blame him if he had?), Alfred had come, by the last ten years of his life, to regard battles and campaigns as a distraction from the proper duties of kingship.

In the preface he wrote to St Augustine's *Soliloquies*, the weary but still indomitable King wrote his own epitaph. In homely parable form Alfred of Wessex, founder of the English kingdom, wistfully explains what he had tried to do since the burden of kingship had been thrust on him in 871:

> Then I gathered for myself staves and props and bars, and handles for all the tools I knew how to use, and crossbars and beams for all the structures which I knew how to build, the fairest pieces of timber, as many as I could carry. I neither came home with a single load, nor did it suit me to bring home all the wood, even if I could have carried it. In each tree I saw something that I required at home. For I advise each of those who is strong and has many wagons, to plan to go to the same wood where I cut these props,

and fetch for himself more there, and load his wagons with fair rods, so that he can plait many a fine wall, and put up many a peerless building, and build a fair enclosure with them; and may dwell therein pleasantly and at his ease winter and summer, as I have not yet done. But he who advised me, to whom the wood was pleasing, may bring it to pass that I shall dwell at greater ease both in this transitory habitation by this road while I am in this world, and also in the eternal home which he has promised us . . .

Alfred died on 26 October 899, in about his fiftieth year; 'he had held the kingdom for one-and-a-half years less than thirty,' notes the *Chronicle*, 'and then his son Edward succeeded to the kingdom.'

3 Edward 'the Elder'
899-924

ALFRED DIED LEAVING ONE vital question open: the succession. Having grown up in the confusion caused by his own father's attempts to dole out the kingdom among the athelings, Alfred had no intention of bequeathing a similar mess. He confined the terms of his will to property settlements, the property being his own and that of his predecessor Ethelred (who had died intestate) with not a mention of the succession. This was deliberate. Alfred was doing justice to his family and to his people for the last time; the new king would be elected fairly, in traditional style, by the councillors of the kingdom who were left free to make their own choice from the members of the ancient line of Cerdic.

There were two contenders: Alfred's son Edward and the atheling Aethelwold, son of Alfred's elder brother Ethelred. Edward first appears in the great war of 892-6, leading the eastern division of Alfred's army. He covered himself with glory in the 893 campaign, driving an invading Danish force back across the Thames, blockading it on an island and receiving its surrender after being reinforced from London by Ethelred of Mercia. With splendid service like this on his record, Edward was the natural choice as Alfred's successor.

Aethelwold, by contrast, seems to have had a flair for political and moral suicide. He made no attempt to eclipse or even rival his cousin's glory, despite the plentiful opportunities provided by the long war of 892-6. Having been disappointed in the election, his next move should have been to make himself Edward's most loyal lieutenant, which would have given Aethelwold every chance of becoming king if anything had happened to Edward; but he threw it all away at the outset by branding himself as a traitor and criminal. He defied Edward by seizing the royal residence of Wimborne and abducting a nun. When Edward besieged Aethelwold in Wimborne, the rebel atheling said 'that he would either live there or die there'; then he abandoned his loyal retainers, sneaking away by night and fleeing to the Danes of Northumbria. The Northumbrian Danes, to whom any feuding amid the formidable Englishmen of the south was naturally welcome, recognized Aethelwold as the rightful king of Wessex and promised him support.

Edward therefore took up the reins of power with the 'establishment' of Wessex and English Mercia rallying to his side indignantly, but faced with an invasion in the near future that would probably be headed by his renegade cousin. This gave him enough time to agree on a defence strategy with Ethelred of Mercia, making sure that the defences of the burhs were kept in prime condition and briefing the ealdormen to be ready for an instant call-up as soon as the blow fell.

With the accession of Edward the new kingdom of England was quietly, almost casually proclaimed. One of Edward's first decisions as king was to take the step at which Alfred had hesitated, and style himself 'King of the Anglo-Saxons'. He seems to have done this naturally, with no thunder from Olympus or protests from Ethelred that Mercia, at least, owed no traditional allegiance to Wessex and its kings. The new royal title first appears in a land grant of 901 in which Edward, 'by the gift of God's grace king of the Anglo-Saxons', deeds a tract of land in Wessex 'free in all things, except the fortification of fortresses [burhs] and the construction of bridges and military service'. This, like Alfred's treaty with Guthrum some fifteen years earlier, remains a key document in the early history of the English kingdom; the land grant in question concerned territory in Wessex only, but the royal title used by Edward assumed authority over every Englishman in the island.

Aethelwold's invasion came in 902. Edward and Ethelred had no choice but to sit tight and wait for Aethelwold to make his move – he had too many possible approach-routes for all to be blocked. He might have tested the strength of the new partnership between Wessex and English Mercia by leaving the Mercians alone and concentrating on Wessex; instead, typically, Aethelwold did the one thing guaranteed to bind the Mercians and West Saxons closer together. He landed in Essex and persuaded King Eohric, Guthrum's successor, to rampage all over English Mercia. The Danes broke into Wessex at Cricklade on the upper Thames and reached the Berkshire Downs before swinging north-east for home. While this was going on, Edward led his own army on a counter-raid deep into Danish territory – the first time an English army had crossed the frontier since its negotiation by Alfred and Guthrum back in the 880s – and harried the Danish settlements as far north as the Fens.

The *Chronicle* makes it clear that Edward was not seeking

battle with the Danish army; this was a punitive strike, to demonstrate that from now on Danish infringements of the peace would be heavily avenged on Danish territory. Edward had already begun his retreat and was urging the lagging Kentish contingent to join up when the Kentishmen were intercepted by the returning Danish army. In the resultant hard-fought 'battle of the Holme' the Kentishmen suffered heavy losses, but more than atoned for their earlier insubordination by killing Aethelwold, King Eohric and most of the Danish war-leaders. At one stroke, Edward's rival had been eliminated and the menace of the East Anglian Danes temporarily dispelled.

Edward's aggressive handling of the 903 campaign set the tone for the new reign which was, from start to finish, in total contrast to that of his father. Alfred had been the great defender, salvaging as much as he could and making it as secure as possible for his successors. Under Edward, the English went over to the offensive. That they were able to do this barely thirty years after the wreck of Northumbria and Mercia was largely thanks to Alfred, but it also exploited the fact that the initial impetus of Scandinavian conquest had spent itself.

By 904, Edward and Ethelred could appreciate that the Danes in Northumbria, Mercia and East Anglia had become more of a static menace than a dynamic one: but a menace they remained. As the late and unlamented Aethelwold had so conveniently demonstrated, Saxon England's Danish neighbours were willing to march at the behest of an English pretender; their territory would provide a natural and secure beach-head for any future rogue army which might decide to attack England. Edward and Ethelred therefore agreed that merely standing on the defensive would not guarantee their people any genuine security; instead, Danish territory must be pushed back further and further until the surviving Danes either left England or submitted to English rule. Thus Alfred's frontier with the Danes, violated by Aethelwold and his East Anglian allies in 902, must no longer be regarded as an outer defence-line, but as a line from which to embark on the expansion of England.

The frontier followed the natural axis delineated by Watling Street – the English name for the decaying Roman road slicing north-west across England from London to Chester. As agreed in the treaty, the frontier ran 'up the Thames, and then up the

Lea, and along the Lea to its source, then in a straight line to Bedford, then up the Ouse to the Watling Street'. Thanks to Alfred's prescience when negotiating with Guthrum, this gave the English a sizeable bridgehead or enclave east of Watling Street. Edward and Ethelred seem to have started by trying to expand this enclave and create others on the Danish side of Watling Street, using peaceful means. They ordered their ealdormen and thanes whose lands marched with the frontier to buy land from the Danes, cash down. One such purchase, for an outlay of 'ten pounds of gold and silver', secured an area of five 'hides' – the hide being the Saxon unit of land measurement considered sufficient to support one free peasant farmer (*ceorl*) and his household.

By any reckoning, buying land from the national enemy must have appeared a high-risk venture because of the chances of losing both outlay and investment. The purchases would be natural targets for the first Danish attacks in the event of war and, as this compulsory land purchase programme was in effect a wealth tax, it was probably highly unpopular. No English land-owner, however wealthy, can have enjoyed being *ordered* to make hefty cash payments in order primarily to increase the recruiting area for national service. Though there is no confirmation from contemporary sources, it is at least possible that Edward's first experiment with expanding the frontier at private expense met with growing opposition. Such opposition would have come from the men he dared not alienate: the ealdormen and thanes who recruited his army and commanded its contingents in time of war.

A period of mounting internal tension and resentment, resulting in an otherwise revered king backing down before some kind of ultimatum from his subjects, would be an interlude best forgotten. That is what seems to have happened to the years 904–8, about which the *Chronicle* is virtually silent. Bishop Denewulf of Winchester, we are told, died in 908. Apart from the Bishop's demise there is only one other entry for 904–8: 906, in which year Edward 'established peace' with the Danish armies of Northumbria and East Anglia. This he did at Tiddingford near Leighton Buzzard – right on the Watling Street frontier – and the northern annal of the *Chronicle* categorically states that Edward settled with the Danes 'from necessity'. But was the 'necessity' for peace external or internal? The only reason for a gifted general and national hero like Edward *not* to take the field against a Danish coalition (unless both he and Ethelred were seriously ill, of which there is no indication) has to be that he was temporarily unable to raise an army. And if he was unable to fight because of trouble from his own ealdormen and thanes on the frontier, no wonder the *Chronicle* omits such a humiliating confession.

Extending this scenario to 909 we would then expect to see Edward, having bought off the Danish coalition and ensured its dispersal, abandoning his land-purchase policy and effecting a reconciliation with his warrior nobility. We might expect king and aristocracy to take the time-honoured way of sinking their differences – a war of aggression against the common enemy. And that is precisely what we find in the *Chronicle's* entry for 909, bringing the sterile years since Aethelwold's defeat to a close:

> King Edward sent an army both from the West Saxons and from the Mercians, and it ravaged very severely the territory of the northern army, both men and all kinds of cattle, and they killed many men of those Danes, and were five weeks there.

So began the great years of the Reconquest: a decade and a half of relentless advance and consolidation by the West Saxons and Mercians, ending with Edward master of all England south of the Humber. In 909 Edward was still no more than the acknowledged king of all free Englishmen living south-west of the Danish frontier negotiated by Alfred. When Edward died in 924, however, the quasi-independence of Mercia had passed into history together with Alfred's frontier. King not only of Wessex and the south-east but of East Anglia and Mercia as well, Edward had brought into being a united 'kingdom of England' which neither Alfred nor any of the earlier Bretwaldas would have recognized.

It is typical of the English that the humiliating Norman Conquest of 1066 remains the best-remembered event in their history, while the glorious English Reconquest of Edward, 150 years earlier, remains sunk in almost total oblivion. The Reconquest was a series of military operations without parallel in early medieval warfare, ranking Edward with the greatest of

England's warrior kings. Battle and manoeuvre were supplemented by a highly intelligent use of geography and well-sited fortifications. There is an uncanny similarity between Edward's campaigns and those of Gnaeus Agricola, the Roman conqueror of northern Britain in the first century AD. It prompts the intriguing speculation (warranted by the absence of any detailed biography of Edward similar to Asser's life of Alfred) that Edward had made good use of the scholars attracted to the West Saxon court by Alfred, and had at least been introduced to Tacitus' life of Agricola.

Edward's *modus operandi* was basically simple. Each year saw a modest advance deeper into Danish territory and the creation of at least one new burh with an English garrison. The new garrisons and the main English field army then collaborated in defeating the nearest Danish army, the process being repeated in the following year. Although Ethelred of Mercia died in 910, Edward continued to enjoy the splendid assistance furnished by his sister Aethelflaed, Ethelred's widow. Taking over from her dead husband with the title 'Lady of the Mercians', Aethelflaed directed the operations of the Mercian army and the siting of new Mercian burhs every bit as successfully as her brother, who was thus left free to concentrate on the reduction of eastern Mercia and East Anglia. Edward advanced on two fronts: a coastal drive in Essex, which the English fleet could support, and an inland advance on the Bedford/Northampton sector.

Until 917 the Danes fought back stoutly, launching fierce but unavailing attacks on the growing network of English burhs. Edward was content to let them wear out their strength on the English frontier defences, and the first summer campaign of 917 saw the familiar pattern repeating itself. The Danish army of Northampton and Leicester assaulted the two new burhs built by Edward that spring, only to be repulsed. The East Anglian Danes briefly joined forces with their Mercian comrades, and were repulsed in turn. Meanwhile Aethelflaed and the English Mercians took Derby after a tough fight, punching a vital link out of the chain of Danish armies stretching from the Peak District south-east into East Anglia. Edward now took the initiative, assembling a scratch force from the frontier burhs which struck at the East Anglian army, storming its fortified camp at Tempsford; '... and they killed the King and Earl

OPPOSITE English troops repairing a *burh* and (BOTTOM) rounding up the local livestock before a siege. Edward's mastery of fortification as an *offensive* strategy marks him as one of the ablest medieval warrior-kings.

72

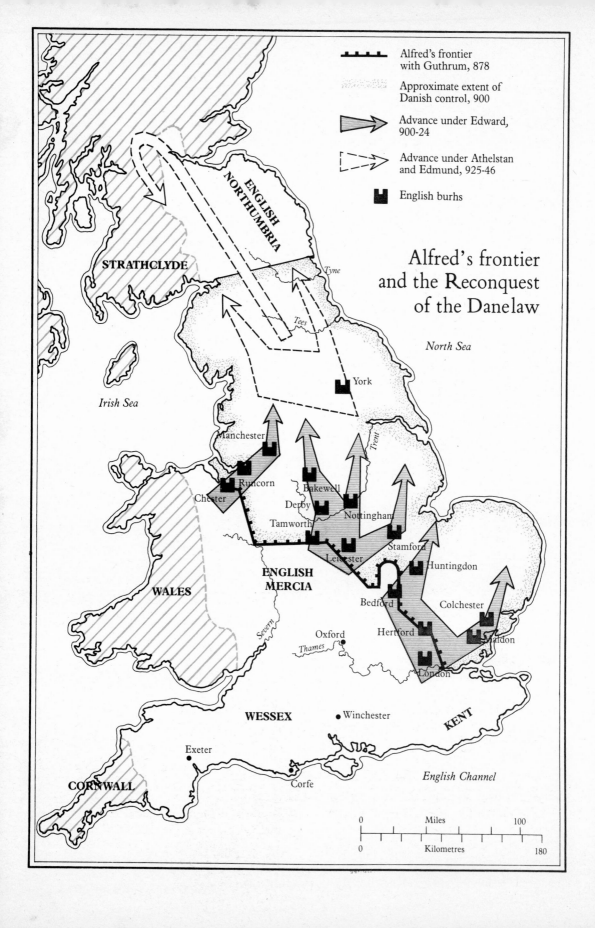

Legend

- **⬛⬛⬛⬛** Alfred's frontier with Guthrum, 878
- Approximate extent of Danish control, 900
- **➤** Advance under Edward, 900-24
- ⇢ Advance under Athelstan and Edmund, 925-46
- ⬛ English burhs

Alfred's frontier and the Reconquest of the Danelaw

STRATHCLYDE

ENGLISH NORTHUMBRIA

Tyne

Tees

North Sea

Irish Sea

York

Manchester

Runcorn

Chester

Bakewell

Derby

Tamworth

Nottingham

Trent

Leicester

Stamford

Huntingdon

WALES

ENGLISH MERCIA

Bedford

Colchester

Severn

Oxford

Hertford

Maldon

Thames

London

WESSEX

• Winchester

KENT

CORNWALL

Exeter

Corfe

English Channel

| 0 | Miles | 100 |
| 0 | Kilometres | 180 |

Toglos and his son Earl Manna, and his brother and all those who were inside and chose to defend themselves.'

As in the 903 campaign, the fortunes of battle had left the East Anglian Danes beaten and leaderless. This time, however, Edward pressed his advantage. A fresh English expeditionary force from Kent, Surrey, Essex and the frontier burhs of the south-east attacked and took Colchester. A despairing Danish counterblow against the English burh at Maldon on the Essex coast was beaten off and put to rout, the Maldon garrison making a sortie to help the field army scatter the demoralized Danes. Edward promptly turned his attention back to the inland sector. He raised the full muster of Wessex – the third fresh English army to take the field in 917 – and concentrated it at Passenham on the Watling Street frontier. This was too much for the Danish army of Northampton under Earl Thurferth, which surrendered to Edward without a fight 'and sought to have him as their lord and protector'.

Edward's goal was now the isolation of the army of Cambridge – the Danish base from which Guthrum's army had marched to the near-destruction of Wessex only forty-one years before. After relieving the West Saxon troops which had cowed the Northampton Danes into submission, Edward lunged thirty miles north-east and took Huntingdon, a noted former base for Danish assaults on the frontier burhs. When the Huntingdon region hastily submitted to Edward, the Cambridge army was cut off from the north-west. The King's final stroke in this extraordinary year of victory was to take the entire army of Wessex forward to Colchester:

> And many people who had been under the rule of the Danes both in East Anglia and in Essex submitted to him; and all the army in East Anglia swore agreement with him, that they would [agree to] all that he would, and would keep peace with all with whom the king wished to keep peace, both at sea and on land. And the army which belonged to Cambridge chose him especially as its lord and protector, and established it with oaths just as he decreed it. (*Anglo-Saxon Chronicle*)

Edward's dazzling generalship in the campaigns of 917 won him the whole of East Anglia and the eastern Midlands. His bewildering shifts and feints, with each new blow being

OPPOSITE The main axes of English advance during the Reconquest under Edward and Athelstan.

delivered by fresh troops, rapidly brought about the general demoralization of the scattered Danish armies, lacking as they did any supreme commander of Edward's calibre. The English King was now confidently delegating command, despatching expeditions to secure key objectives while he stood back and retained a balanced overview of the general military position.

For 918, Edward and Aethelflaed planned the recovery of north-eastern Mercia as far as the Humber – the old Northumbrian border. The year began with Aethelflaed receiving the submission of Leicester and most of the Danish army there, without a fight. The fame of the 'Lady of the Mercians' now stood so high that she received an embassy from York, offering the submission of the Northumbrian capital. However there was no time to act on this momentous offer before Aethelflaed died on 12 June 918, at Tamworth, the burh she had created five years before.

Edward's opening move in 918 had secured the peaceful submission of Stamford on the River Welland, but when he heard of his sister's death he dropped everything and marched on Tamworth to make certain of the allegiance of Mercia. This, the official takeover of Mercia by Wessex, was a breathless moment in the making of England, and it may be no accident that the Wessex-oriented contemporary sources are so offhand about it. As Ethelred and Aethelflaed had left no male heirs, there was a power vacuum; Edward's only serious rival was his niece Aelfwyn. But Edward certainly came to Tamworth with his army 'and occupied the borough', and the presence of the West Saxon king and his troops must have been a powerful deterrent to any Mercian romantics who might have been tempted to vote for Aethelflaed's daughter as their new 'Lady'. In any event, Edward was duly chosen as the new ruler of Mercia; 'All the nation in the land of the Mercians which had been subject to Aetheflaed submitted to him; and the kings in Wales, Hywel, Clydog and Idwal, and all the race of the Welsh, sought to have him as lord.'

Edward wasted no time in showing his new Mercian subjects that he would lead them to victory, as his sister had done. In 919 he marched on Nottingham and took it, but this was only the prelude to an even more historic moment than the merging of Mercia and Wessex. He showed that England was going to be a land where Englishmen and Danes could live together in harmony, not just on opposite sides of an arbitrary frontier, but as fellow citizens and countrymen. Nottingham was the first public demonstration. After capturing the town, Edward 'ordered it to be repaired *and manned both with Englishmen and Danes. And all the people who had settled in Mercia, both Danish and English, submitted to him.*' [Author's italics]

So it was that the Reconquest did not end in the extermination or even expulsion of the beaten Danes, but in a most liberal amnesty and forward-looking spirit. Such a revolutionary attitude towards the erstwhile mortal enemy of Saxon England is proof, if further proof were needed, of Edward's true greatness as a ruler; many of his subjects must have found it hard to stomach. And the new policy also reflects Edward's commonsense economy – inherited from Alfred – with the resources of his kingdom. By encouraging other Danish communities to submit peacefully to English rule, Edward's experiment at Nottingham was really aimed at sparing Wessex and Mercia from a ruinous commitment to permanent war in the north. The fact was that by 918 both Danes and Englishmen were facing a common enemy: Norsemen crossing from Ireland to conquer and settle in Northumbria. Edward not only diagnosed the peril posed by this new alien power in good time, but demonstrated that the English king was the natural patron for every British ruler who felt himself threatened by the Norsemen. In so doing he gave his own conquests the best possible guarantee of permanence.

Edward's last expeditions expanded the English kingdom to the old frontier of Northumbria, making ostentatious use of Mercian forces to liberate Mercian territory. After building a new burh at Thelwall in late 919, Edward sent a second Mercian army up to the frontier line of the Mersey 'to occupy Manchester in Northumbria, and repair and man it'. This commitment of the Mercians to maintaining the northern frontier was accompanied by a piece of political insurance: the transfer of Aelfwyn to Wessex. Her removal was tartly recorded by the supplement to the *Chronicle* known as the *Mercian Register*: 'In this year also the daughter of Ethelred, lord of the Mercians, was deprived of all authority in Mercia and taken into Wessex, three weeks before Christmas.' Here again

Edward was prudent, providing for the security of the Anglo-Danish kingdom he had created by removing the only possible figurehead for an untimely upsurge of Mercian separatism.

In 920, Edward's expansion to the north reached high tide with the new burh at Bakewell in the Peak District, and the *Chronicle* proudly recorded the crowning honour of his reign:

> And then the king of the Scots and all the people of the Scots, and Ragnald, and the sons of Eadwulf and all who live in Northumbria, both English and Danish, Norsemen and others, and also the king of the Strathclyde Welsh and all the Strathclyde Welsh, chose him as father and lord.

Edward 'the Elder', as his people remembered him, died at Farndon in Mercia on 17 July 924. Taking up the tools which Alfred had contrived for the defence of Wessex, Edward had hammered them into weapons for the creation of a new kingdom of England. He had built magnificently on the foundations laid by Alfred. Now it was up to Edward's own sons to maintain their father's creation, and go on to complete the edifice of England with roof and spire.

4
Athelstan

924-939

EDWARD'S SUCCESSOR WAS HIS eldest son, Athelstan, who ruled England for fifteen years. At first sight Athelstan's contribution to the making of England seems a logical extension of the reconstruction carried out by Alfred and the reconquest of Danish-occupied English territory so vehemently begun by Edward. Like Alfred and Edward, Athelstan won high fame as a capable ruler and victorious leader of armies; he, too, was hailed as a champion of the Christian world. Despite the similarity of his achievements with those of his father and grandfather, however, it was Athelstan's personal *style* of kingship that ranked him head and shoulders above them. Reigning in state as no other English king had done since Offa of Mercia, Athelstan gave the raw new English kingdom an aura which it badly needed. This was an investment of power with kingly splendour, a feeling of pride at home and envy from abroad, a sense of national glory by divine right. In a word, Athelstan gave England majesty.

It is easy to take the cynical (and demonstrably incorrect) view that any Saxon king who showered endowments on the Church guaranteed himself a flattering write-up by the churchmen who wrote the chronicles and histories. Athelstan's aura was all his own work; it reflected his personal taste and manners. He saw the maintenance of its lustre as a facet of kingship as essential as the making and enforcement of laws and the defeating of enemies.

Athelstan was unique in that he was the first atheling of the West Saxon ruling house to be deliberately groomed as a potential king of the English. This, surprisingly, was his grandfather's doing – surprisingly, because Alfred habitually avoided creating precedents which might prove embarrassing for posterity. 'He had arranged', asserts William of Malmesbury, 'that [Athelstan] should be brought up in the court of his daughter Aethelflaed and his son-in-law Ethelred; and there, reared by the great care of his aunt and that most famous ealdorman, in expectation of a kingdom, he trampled down and destroyed envy by the glory of his virtues.' In plain English Athelstan, heir to the throne of Wessex, was reared as a Mercian prince. It was a far-sighted gesture which paid dividends when the Mercian councillors cast their votes for the new king after Edward's funeral at Winchester in the late summer of 924.

PREVIOUS PAGES An English king leads his army to victory on the battlefield. Athelstan's triumph at Brunanburh in 937 was remembered as the crowning event of his reign.

82

William of Malmesbury is an important source for Athelstan's reign, during which the *Chronicle* lapses into one of its more uncommunicative moods. It is to William that we owe the story of the sensation at Athelstan's election, when 'a certain Alfred with his seditious supporters' opposed Athelstan's claim with the assertion that Athelstan was illegitimate. This 'political smear campaign' was indignantly rejected by the rest of the councillors, and one of Athelstan's first acts as king was reportedly to have Alfred sent to Rome for trial (where he most satisfactorily dropped dead while swearing a false oath on St Peter's altar).

The description of Athelstan furnished by William of Malmesbury seems to have been typical of members of the West Saxon royal family: '... not beyond what is becoming in stature, and slender in body; his hair, as we ourselves have seen from his relics, flaxen, beautifully mingled with gold threads.' Athelstan was in his prime when he succeeded Edward – thirty years old – and had three surviving younger brothers, Edwin, Edmund and Eadred. This freed him of the absolute necessity to marry and produce heirs, and he may well have devoted himself to a celibate life from religious motives as well. For Athelstan was an intensely pious man, noted for his avid collecting of sacred relics. This was by no means a private hobby, like the art collection 700 years later of the Stuart king, Charles I; it was an immense national asset, giving Athelstan the special goodwill not only of the Church in England but of every corner of the Christian world community owing spiritual allegiance to Rome. The English king's piety lubricated diplomatic exchanges, encouraged the advancement of art and culture in England and stimulated the pilgrim traffic (medieval forerunner of the modern tourist industry) with the resultant financial benefit to the host country.

Athelstan was also blessed in a more practical sense, from a king's point of view, with four beautiful sisters eagerly sought in marriage by every leading power in western Europe. In 926, Eadhild, the most beautiful sister, was married to Hugh, Duke of the Franks, after a diplomatic mission which had brought gifts of unprecedented magnificence to England. These gifts included the sword of Constantine the Great with one of the nails from the Cross set in its hilt, the lance which had pierced

Evocative of the wealth
of religious art associated
with Athelstan's reign:
the 'Rupert Cross', which
once stood on an altar,
and, from a hoard
discovered at Trewiddle,
a silver chalice originally
gilded inside.

Christ's side on the Cross (a former heirloom of Charlemagne), and fragments of the Cross and Crown of Thorns gorgeously mounted in crystal. Another sister, Edith, married the eldest son of the Holy Roman Emperor Henry 'the Fowler', Prince Otto. These successful transactions by Athelstan are an impressive contrast to Offa of Mercia's failure to reach agreement with Charlemagne (*p. 34*). For 600 years, until the Reformation, many English kings were to angle for marriage settlements with the rulers of the Holy Roman Empire, but few matched the status and success enjoyed by Athelstan in the early years of the kingdom.

One of the sisters was, however, reserved for a marriage aimed at furthering Athelstan's interests in northern England. In the last five years of Edward's reign, the Irish Norsemen had conquered York from the Danes and set up a formidable new kingdom. Along with the other northern rulers its first king, Ragnald, had submitted to Edward in 920, but he had died the following year and the kingdom of York had passed to his cousin Sihtric. Though Sihtric never made formal submission to Edward he wasted no time in opening negotiations with Athelstan for a marriage alliance with the English king. After diplomatic preliminaries including, presumably, Sihtric's instruction and conversion to Christianity, Sihtric went to Tamworth at the end of January 926 and the marriage ceremony took place.

Athelstan seems to have hoped that this remarkable piece of dynasticism (which would hardly have been possible even ten years before) would in time bring the kingdom of York peacefully within England's orbit, as the marriage of his aunt Aethelflaed had led to the merging of Wessex and Mercia; but it was not to be. By the spring of 927 Sihtric – no doubt worried about maintaining his authority over his heathen warrior Norsemen subjects – had relapsed into heathenism; '. . . and after a short while', as Roger of Wendover puts it, Sihtric 'ended his life miserably as an apostate'.

The Norsemen of York promptly elected as their new king Olaf, Sihtric's son by a former marriage. Olaf Sihtricsson received immediate support from his uncle Guthfrith, King of the Norsemen in Ireland, who crossed to England with an army. Athelstan's response to this menacing development was to move in hard and fast with the English army, invading Northumbria and marching on York. The campaign was a spectacular success. The Norsemen were scattered, Guthfrith fleeing north to seek asylum in Scotland and Olaf escaping to Ireland, leaving Athelstan master of southern Northumbria. He followed up this initial triumph by marching north into the kingdom of Strathclyde, as Edward had advanced to Bakewell in 920, and summoning the northern kings to submit. At the same time, Constantine of Scotland was ordered to hand over Guthfrith; but as Constantine headed for the rendezvous at Eamont, near Penrith, Guthfrith escaped (possibly with Constantine's connivance). He headed south to raise what forces he could at York.

The three kings who made their formal submission to Athelstan at Eamont on 12 July 927 were Constantine of Scotland, Owain of Gwent, and Hywel of Strathclyde; the rulers of the Celtic north-west of Britain for the first time paying homage to an English king in their territory, on his terms and at a place named by him. But the Eamont 'conference' was a climacteric for another reason. Over the previous fifty years, since the Great Army of the Danes had divided and settled in prostrate Northumbria, a defiant enclave of free Northumbrians had held out far north of the Tyne, based on the stronghold of Bamburgh. They obeyed hereditary leaders known as 'high-reeves', the first of whom, Eadwulf, had enjoyed Alfred's friendship and support and ruled at Bamburgh until 913. In July 927, Ealdred, son of Eadwulf, came to Eamont to make his submission to Alfred's grandson – the ruler of free Northumbria accepting the ruler of the southern English as overlord.

We can identify three crucial moments in the creation of the English kingdom. The first had been the rally of the southern English and their submission to Alfred after his capture of London, back in 886. The second was the submission of the Mercians to Edward in 918; and this, the submission of Ealdred to Athelstan, was the third. Barely half a century after Alfred's humiliating flight to Athelney to escape Guthrum's army, the ruler of Wessex reigned over a multi-national kingdom stretching from the Channel to the Scots border. As yet its central and northern provinces, whose strongest traditions were

OPPOSITE Athelstan's conquest of Danish Northumbria completed the foundation of the English kingdom. Here the king presents a copy of Bede's works to the patron saint of the north, St Cuthbert.

86

those of independent kingdoms, were held together only by the frailest of stitches. Athelstan now set himself confidently not only to make this precarious realm secure, but to administer and govern it as a coherent entity.

He started in 928 by heading south and shattering Guthfrith's hopes of reviving the Norse kingdom of York. After another brief campaign Guthfrith's forces were scattered; he himself was brought prisoner to Athelstan, lavishly entertained for four days – then allowed to return to Ireland. The Norse defences of York were razed to the ground to deter further challenges to Athelstan's authority. An impressive hoard of treasure was removed from the Norse stronghold, and Athelstan made a point of having this shared out among the English army. With the north secure and a victorious and enthusiastic army at his back, Athelstan now turned west. Some time between 927 and 931 he broke down the resistance of the kings of Wales – the rulers of Dyfed, Gwynedd, Morgannwg, Gwent and Brycheiniog – and summoned the apprehensive monarchs to a meeting at Hereford. Their submission was received along with an agreement to pay an annual tribute to Athelstan of twenty pounds of gold, 300 pounds of silver, 25,000 oxen, and 'as many as he chose' of hounds and hawks – a tribute so great as to be unprecedented.

Having settled the River Wye as the southern frontier between England and Wales, Athelstan made an expedition into the West Country. Here the problem was easterly expansion through south Devon by the old enemies of Wessex: the 'West Welsh' of Cornwall, who had flourished to the extent that they inhabited Exeter on equal terms with the English. Instead of using diplomacy Athelstan treated the Cornishmen to a bruising pogrom, expelling them from Exeter and their other settlements in Devon and driving them west beyond the Tamar. But the river was more of a territorial marker than a terminal frontier between England and Cornwall; Athelstan followed up his resettlement of the 'West Welsh' by founding a bishopric for them west of the Tamar, at St Germans.

Having delineated his frontiers, Athelstan tackled the problem of ruling on terms which would be accepted as fair by all his subjects – West Saxons, Mercians, East Anglians, Danes, Norsemen and Northumbrian English alike. Not even Edward

88

had faced a task of this magnitude, and we have many useful clues to how Athelstan went about it because many of his charters, unlike those of his father, have survived. These charters are very different from the spartan transactions of earlier English kings, normally witnessed by the local Church leaders and ealdormen and possibly half a dozen thanes of the royal household. When Athelstan made a land grant or conferred a privilege, the confirming charter was deliberately composed as a solemn act of state. Athelstan clearly encouraged his clerks not to stint themselves when pronouncing the conventional curse on future violators of his charters:

> If, however – which God forbid – anyone puffed up with the pride of arrogance shall try to destroy or infringe this little document of my agreement and confirmation, let him know that on the last and fearful day of assembly, when the trumpet of the archangel is clanging the call and bodies are leaving the foul graveyards, he will burn with Judas the commiter of impious treachery and also with the miserable Jews, blaspheming with sacrilegious mouth Christ on the altar of the Cross, in eternal confusion in the devouring flames of blazing torments in punishment without end.

or when extolling the King's piety and munificence:

> Truly the record of this our intention, by the inspiration, favour and help of our God and Lord Jesus Christ, was written in the year of our Lord's incarnation 930, and in the sixth year of the reign committed to me, the seventh indiction, the third epact, the second concurrent, 7 June, the twenty-first day of the moon, in the city well known to all which is called Nottingham, all the body of chief men rejoicing, under the wings of royal generosity. The authority also of its unshaken firmness was strengthened by these witnesses, whose names are entered below depicted with letters.

This particular charter ratifies Athelstan's grant of Amounderness (that region of Lancashire nowadays traversed by the M6 motorway north of Preston) to the archbishopric of York. Athelstan's own title is no less grandiose than the language used throughout: 'I, Athelstan, King of the English, elevated by the right hand of the Almighty, which is Christ, to the throne of the whole kingdom of Britain.' But apart from the florid 'officialese' of its style, the Amounderness charter proves that the

King's ambitious claim to be 'King of Britain' was not without substance. To transact the royal business at Nottingham of which the Amounderness charter formed part, Athelstan had summoned every important lay and clerical magnate in the island. When in 901 Edward the Elder had made the land grant mentioned on *p. 67*, he had had it witnessed by his younger brother Aethelweard, eleven ealdormen and twenty-two king's thanes – not a single churchman among them. Athelstan's Amounderness charter, by contrast, was witnessed by the archbishops of Canterbury and York, three Welsh sub-kings, seven English ealdormen and six Danish earls, ten king's thanes, and thirteen other worthies for whom no ranks are given. This was government in the grand manner, with the King attended by the magnates of his entire realm and its neighbouring client powers. It was the stately ancestor of the Parliament of England: the Saxon *Witena gemot* or 'meeting of the wise', the Witan of England without which the king could not govern.

As documented, Athelstan's style of government shows the dual nationality of the English kingdom already constructively at work – the Christian successors to the terrible Danish earls of the Great Army lining up with English ealdormen to make their crosses on state documents. Athelstan initiated no revolutionary new framework of administration, but he considerably extended the system adapted by Alfred and Edward from the rubble of the heptarchy. This system survived the Reconquest because it worked. The king's authority was seconded by the archbishop of York in the north and by the archbishop of Canterbury in the south. In Wessex, the regional ealdormen were more or less 'paired' with the bishops of the southern sees. Essex, East Anglia and Mercia west of Watling Street were governed by English ealdormen. East of Watling Street the Danish territory generally known as the 'Danelaw' was administered by Danish earls, whose spheres of authority were centered on the towns which had been the bases for the Danish armies conquered by Edward and Aethelflaed.

Athelstan was lavish with his law codes, of which no less than six were issued in his reign, deepening and extending the vital principle established by Alfred in his treaty with Guthrum: that Englishmen and Danes were to be equal in law. Athelstan

sought to crack down on theft, crimes of violence, and violations of religious observance (trading on Sunday being particularly frowned upon). Perjury was clearly no less of a problem; under Athelstan, a perjurer was not only to lose his right to 'clearance' from accusation by oath, but was condemned to be buried in unconsecrated ground when he died 'unless he has the witness of the bishop in whose diocese he is that he has done penance for it as his confessor has prescribed for him'. The burhs created during the Reconquest and under Alfred still had to have their fortifications kept in order, and all repairs had to be completed 'by a fortnight after Rogation day'

Tenth-century English manuscript shows the king and his council. Today the Sword of State is still carried when an English monarch opens a new session of Parliament.

91

in order to be ready every year, by the end of May at the latest, for possible trouble. But the original, purely military function of the burhs was being supplemented by their role as focal points for peaceful commerce, and Athelstan sought to accelerate the process. He ordered that there was to be one coinage for the whole kingdom, and that minting was to be carried out only in specified towns. (Crooked minters had the hand which had committed the crime cut off and stuck up on the mint.) In addition, Athelstan banned all buying and selling outside towns, this measure alone giving a tremendous boost to the development of the English town.

These examples go to show that Athelstan, beneath all the pomp and circumstance with which he cloaked his kingship, was a ruler of immense energy, ability and forethought. Yet despite these much-needed qualities, England was no oasis of peace during his reign. We do not know, for instance, what on earth lay behind the sinister entry for 933 made by the northern chronicler Simeon of Durham: 'King Athelstan ordered his brother Edwin to be drowned at sea.' Edwin certainly *was* drowned in 933, shipwrecked while crossing the Channel to Flanders; the chronicler of St Bertin's monastery, which buried the dead atheling, cautiously states that Edwin had been 'driven by some disturbance in his kingdom'. Edwin may have been expelled from England for identifying himself with some opposition faction, for William of Malmesbury, searching for more compliments to pay his hero, mentions that Athelstan was 'a thunderbolt to rebels by his invincible steadfastness'. Certainly the monks of St Bertin's did well out of giving Edwin Christian burial, for Athelstan 'sent several gifts to this place as alms for him'.

Nor has any explanation survived of why, in 934, Athelstan marched into Scotland with his full army, supported by his fleet. It was obviously a move to cure King Constantine of recent or imminent unfriendly behaviour, rather than an attempt at outright conquest. Constantine made no attempt to stand and fight; the English army advanced almost as far as Aberdeen, plundering as it went, while the crews of the fleet enjoyed themselves by ravaging the Scottish coast all the way north to Caithness. Athelstan may have come to realize that the Irish Norsemen were very far from being a spent force, and that

Athelstan the warrior. This fanciful scene shows him in youth during his father's wars, capturing a Danish chief. When he became king, none of the splendid state he maintained detracted from the king's time-honoured role as supreme war-leader.

Constantine was their natural ally on British soil. But if his punishment of the Scots in 934 was intended as a long-term deterrent, it failed completely.

Three years later the English kingdom was faced with a deadly combination of northern foes: a Norse expeditionary force from Ireland assisted in strength by Constantine and the King of Strathclyde. Constantine was naturally eager to avenge his recent humiliation at Athelstan's hands; a similar motive existed for the King of the Norsemen, Olaf, son of Guthfrith, whom Athelstan had pulled down from the throne

93

Scene from the twelfth-century Bury Bible shows God assisting the English cause in an assault on a town during Athelstan's wars.

of York and driven out of England. The outcome of this joint assault on Northumbria made Athelstan a living legend for the Old English. Somewhere between the Mersey and the Solway, at a place called 'Brunanburh', Athelstan and his brother Edmund led a West Saxon and Mercian army to glorious victory over their enemies. All we know of Brunanburh is that it was a day-long, bruising fight from which the enemy kings escaped with the wrecks of their armies. It was inconclusive. It did no more than scotch a threat which materialized again with stunning effect only two years later; but, for the English, Brunanburh was hailed as an epic worthy of undying memory. The *Chronicle* itself – as it had never done for the victories of Alfred or Edward – recorded the victory in ringing epic verse:

> In this year King Athelstan, lord of nobles, dispenser of treasure to men, and his brother also, Edmund atheling, won by the sword's edge undying glory in battle round Brunanburh. Edward's sons

94

clove the shield-wall, hewed the linden-wood shields with hammered swords, for it was natural to men of their lineage to defend their land, their treasure and their homes, in frequent battle against every foe...

The whole day long the West Saxons with mounted companies kept in pursuit of the hostile peoples, grievously they cut down the fugitives from behind with their whetted swords. The Mercians refused not hard conflict to any men who with Olaf had sought this land in the bosom of a ship over the tumult of waters, coming doomed to the fight. Five young kings lay on that field of battle, slain by the swords, and also seven of Olaf's earls, and a countless host of seamen and Scots. There the prince of the Norsemen was put to flight, driven perforce to the prow of his ship with a small company; the vessel pressed on in the water, the king set out over the fallow flood and saved his life.

There also the aged Constantine ... the grey-haired warrior, the old and wily one, had no cause to vaunt of that sword clash; no more had Olaf...

Then the Norsemen, the sorry survivors from the spears, put out in their studded ships ... to make for Dublin across the deep water, back to Ireland humbled in heart. Also the two brothers, king and atheling, returned together to their own country, the land of the West Saxons, exulting in the battle. ... Never yet in this island before this, by what books tell us and our ancient sages, was a greater slaughter of a host made by the edge of the sword, since the Angles and Saxons came hither from the east, invading Britain over the broad seas, and the proud assailants, warriors eager for glory, overcame the Britons and won a country.

Brunanburh was inevitably remembered as the crowning event of Athelstan's splendid reign. When he died at Gloucester on 27 October 939, Athelstan's achievement was secure. He had rounded out the creation of the kingdom of England, going on to show how it could be defended, justly and efficiently ruled, and raised to the highest honour in the eyes of the world. No ruler, in any age, can hope to do more. Athelstan had set a standard of English kingship which any of his successors would be proud to attain or even approach, and which triumphantly survived the troubles which fell upon the kingdom after his death.

UNTIL THE TIME OF Athelstan's death in 939 the English were lucky in that Alfred, Edward and Athelstan had all reigned long enough to give their realms a fair measure of continuity, and to allow vital tap-roots to grow. After Athelstan, however, came three short reigns within twenty years. It was a period of crisis and change in which the younger sons of Edward, worthily emulating their grandfather Alfred, met and finally thwarted the last attempts by Norse kings to conquer northern England.

Athelstan's successor was Edmund, only eighteen years old but, like his late brother, full of renown for his prowess on the field of Brunanburh two years before. The strategic emptiness of that battle was now revealed, for the new king was at once faced with another invasion from Ireland by Olaf Guthfrithson. Olaf had clearly learned a good deal from the fiasco of 937. In the year of Brunanburh the Norsemen, after landing, had tarried in Lancashire in order to join forces with the troops of Scotland and Strathclyde; but this had only given Athelstan and Edmund time to raise their own forces and march north to intercept the invaders. Olaf made no such error in the autumn of 939. Almost certainly waiting for news of the great Athelstan's death, and the ensuing concentration of the English magnates at Kingston-on-Thames for the election and conse-cration of the new king, Olaf swept across the Irish Sea, landed, and marched straight on York in an irresistible *coup de main*. By the end of the year he was king of York, with both Northumbria and northern Mercia at his mercy.

The far-sightedness of Athelstan, in ordering that the fortifi-cations of the English burhs were to be kept in good order, was soon justified. In 940 Olaf marched south across the Humber into the provinces recovered by Edward in the last years of the Reconquest. He was accompanied by Archbishop Wulfstan of York, who was to support every attempt to found an independent kingdom in his province for the next twelve years. Wulfstan had clearly decided that England should properly consist of two kingdoms, north and south, corresponding to the archiepiscopal sees of York and Canterbury; he wanted to see Northumbria securely under Norse rule, with himself the spiritual overlord of the northern kingdom. His efforts to bring about the tidy partition of Athelstan's kingdom reflect the

Proof of Scandinavian
influences at work in
tenth-century Saxon
England: a silver disc
brooch clumsily tries to
copy the coiled energy of
Viking art forms.

natural resentment of many provincial magnates at being
subject to the beck and call of an English king hundreds of miles
away.

In 940 Olaf started by besieging Northampton, but the
English garrison beat his army off. He thereupon turned north-
west, attacked Tamworth, stormed it, and ravaged the surrounding country. This success seems to have convinced many
that the Norsemen had come to stay. By the time that Olaf and
Wulfstan reached and took Leicester, Edmund was approaching with the English army; but the Northumbrians had already
renounced their allegiance to him. Then Earl Orm, overlord of
the Danelaw's 'Five Boroughs' of Leicester, Nottingham,
Derby, Stamford and Lincoln, declared for Olaf. Edmund did
all he could to stop the rot spreading. He besieged Olaf and
Wulfstan in Leicester; '... and he could have subdued them',
comments the *Chronicle*, 'if they had not escaped by night from

the borough'. At this point the archbishops of Canterbury and York intervened and negotiated a peace settlement between Olaf and Edmund. This amounted to the biggest humiliation suffered by an English king in over sixty-three years – since Alfred's flight to Athelney – for the peace left the land of the Five Boroughs subject to Olaf. More than twenty years of English rule between Watling Street and the Humber came to a brief end with this shaming settlement.

The luck of the English held, however, for Olaf, having proved himself a most dangerous and wily opponent, was dead by the end of 941. His last campaign, earlier that year, had been a harrying expedition to the far north of Northumbria – which shows that the Northumbrians of Bamburgh, at least, had not forgotten their long years of resistance to the Danes and had remained loyal to Edmund. Olaf Guthfrithson was replaced as king of York by his cousin Olaf Sihtricsson, who turned out to be far less formidable. In 942 Edmund led the English army into the land of the Five Boroughs and recovered it with ease. Earl Orm's treachery two years before had been little more than an exercise in power politics at the top, and Edmund found himself hailed as a liberator by the Danish population. The importance of this was commemorated by another burst of poetry in the *Chronicle*:

> In this year King Edmund, lord of the English, protector of men, the beloved performer of mighty deeds, overran Mercia, as bounded by Dore, Whitwell gate and the broad stream, the River Humber; and five boroughs, Leicester and Lincoln, Nottingham and likewise Stamford, and also Derby. The Danes were previously subjected by force under the Norsemen, and for a long time in bonds of captivity to the heathens, until the defender of warriors, the son of Edward, King Edmund, redeemed them, to his glory.

The archbishops' subsequent peace included Olaf's acceptance of baptism, with Edmund himself acting as godfather. It must have seemed to Wulfstan that his hopes for an independent Northumbria were close to realization, but he had reckoned without the intolerance of Norse armies towards unsuccessful leaders. By the end of 943, Olaf had been deposed as king of York and replaced by Raegnald Guthfrithson. He too was briefly recognized by Edmund and a second diplomatic

OPPOSITE The tenth-century *Benedictional of St Aethelwold* is the most accomplished and celebrated of the beautiful manuscripts of the Winchester school of illumination. This page shows the Annunciation.

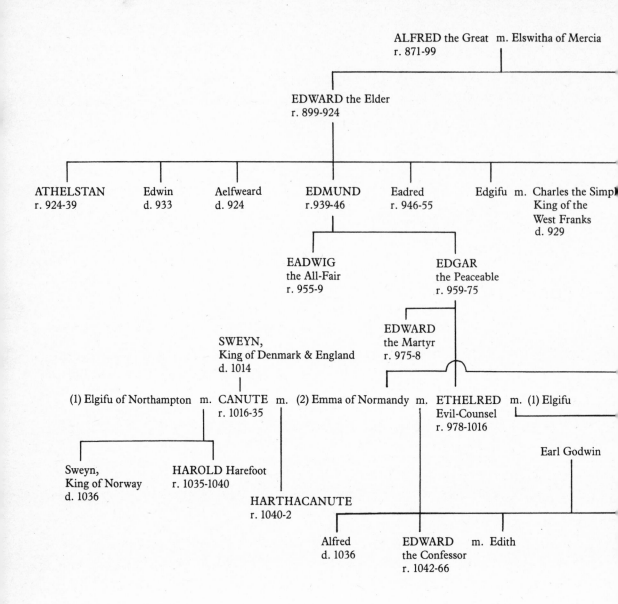

ALFRED the Great m. Elswitha of Mercia
r. 871-99

EDWARD the Elder
r. 899-924

ATHELSTAN r. 924-39 | Edwin d. 933 | Aelfweard d. 924 | EDMUND r.939-46 | Eadred r. 946-55 | Edgifu m. Charles the Simpl King of the West Franks d. 929

EADWIG the All-Fair r. 955-9

EDGAR the Peaceable r. 959-75

EDWARD the Martyr r. 975-8

SWEYN, King of Denmark & England d. 1014

(1) Elgifu of Northampton m. CANUTE m. (2) Emma of Normandy m. ETHELRED Evil-Counsel r. 978-1016 m. (1) Elgifu
r. 1016-35

Earl Godwin

Sweyn, King of Norway d. 1036

HAROLD Harefoot r. 1035-1040

HARTHACANUTE r. 1040-2

Alfred d. 1036

EDWARD the Confessor r. 1042-66 m. Edith

The descent from Alfred the Great to Henry II

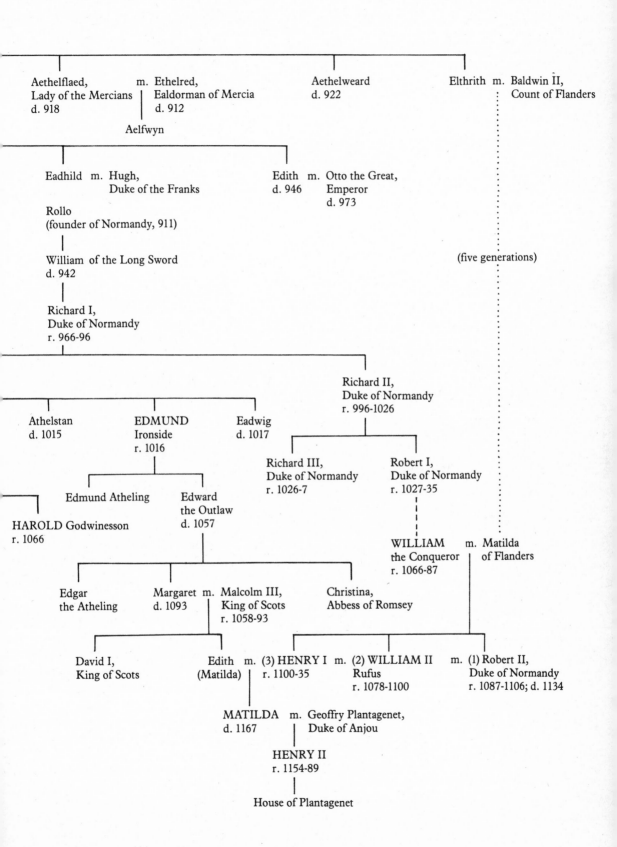

Aethelflaed,　m. Ethelred,
Lady of the Mercians　Ealdorman of Mercia
d. 918　d. 912

Aethelweard
d. 922

Elthrith　m.　Baldwin II,
Count of Flanders

Aelfwyn

Eadhild　m. Hugh,
Duke of the Franks

Edith　m. Otto the Great,
d. 946　Emperor
d. 973

Rollo
(founder of Normandy, 911)

(five generations)

William of the Long Sword
d. 942

Richard I,
Duke of Normandy
r. 966-96

Richard II,
Duke of Normandy
r. 996-1026

Athelstan
d. 1015

EDMUND
Ironside
r. 1016

Eadwig
d. 1017

Richard III,
Duke of Normandy
r. 1026-7

Robert I,
Duke of Normandy
r. 1027-35

Edmund Atheling

Edward
the Outlaw
d. 1057

HAROLD Godwinesson
r. 1066

WILLIAM　m. Matilda
the Conqueror　of Flanders
r. 1066-87

Edgar
the Atheling

Margaret m. Malcolm III,
d. 1093　King of Scots
r. 1058-93

Christina,
Abbess of Romsey

David I,
King of Scots

Edith　m. (3) HENRY I m. (2) WILLIAM II　m. (1) Robert II,
(Matilda)　r. 1100-35　Rufus　Duke of Normandy
r. 1078-1100　r. 1087-1106; d. 1134

MATILDA　m. Geoffry Plantagenet,
d. 1167　Duke of Anjou

HENRY II
r. 1154-89

House of Plantagenet

Sequel to the battle scene
on pages 80–1: the
victorious king, still
holding his spear, inspects
the prisoners of war.

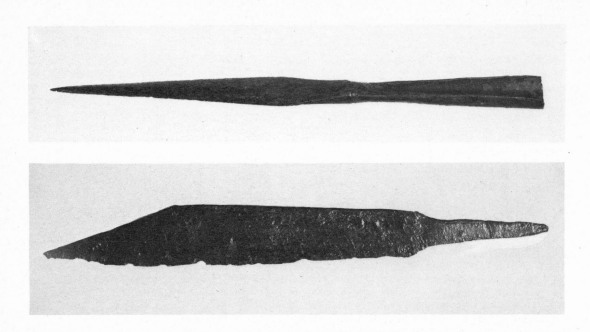

Relics of the wars; a spearhead (TOP) and an English *seax*, the distinctive one-edged chopping sword.

christening was performed; but the English king was only playing for time. Edmund had no intention of resting content with the recovery of the kingdom built up by his father; he was determined to restore the England of Athelstan.

Having become godfather to two successive Norse kings of York, Edmund crossed the Humber in 944 and drove both of them clean out of England. Northumbria remained subject to Edmund for the rest of his brief reign, but the King had not forgotten the vulnerability of the northern province and the danger of Scotland and Strathclyde helping future Norse invaders, as they had in the year of Brunanburh. Edmund's solution to the 'northern question' was that elegant ploy of *realpolitik* – playing off one party against the other. In 945 Edmund ravaged Strathclyde, then granted it to Malcolm of Scotland in return for a treaty of alliance. This proved far more effective in securing the northern border than Athelstan's sledge-hammer invasion ten years before. Edmund's cunning cession of Strathclyde to the Scots ensured Saxon England over half a century of peace with Scotland, and was one of the most impressive masterstrokes of diplomacy achieved by any of the Saxon kings.

Although he ruled for only six and a half years and died while still in his middle twenties, Edmund was remembered by the

106

Old English as one of the greatest of their kings. This was partly due to his share in the glory of Brunanburh, and partly because he died in a most honourable way: on 26 May 946, while going to the help of one of his officers who was being attacked by a felon with a dagger. But above all Edmund was remembered for the energy and speed with which he ousted the Norsemen and restored his brother's kingdom. Had he lived, Edmund would certainly have matched Athelstan in dignity and authority, if not in personal style and splendour. Like his brother, Edmund was a generous patron of the Church – and a good picker of men. He launched the career of one of the most influential churchmen in English history when he appointed Dunstan abbot of Glastonbury in 943.

The youngest son of Edward the Elder, Edmund's brother Eadred, was the new king, and he proved himself no less able than Athelstan and Edmund had been before him. It seems that, on hearing the news of Edmund's murder, Archbishop Wulfstan made another play for an independent Northumbria, for Eadred's first act as king was immediately to 'reduce all Northumbria under his rule'. He took the opportunity to renew the Scottish alliance secured by Edmund, for 'the Scots swore oaths to him that they would agree to all he wanted'. In 947 Eadred went to Tanshelf, near Pontefract, and repeated the process with the magnates of Northumbria; '. . . and there', comments the *Chronicle* sourly, 'Archbishop Wulfstan and all the councillors of the Northumbrians pledged themselves to the King, and within a short space they were false to it all, both pledge and oaths as well.'

The reason for this latest disaffection on the part of the Northumbrians was the sudden arrival of one of the most colourful characters of the later Viking era: Eric 'Bloodaxe' of Norway. Despite his ferocious nickname and a spectacular career of raids and battles, Eric's trouble was that he had been born a century too late – very like Penda of Mercia three hundred years before, who had represented the last of the sixth-century fighting pagan kings in the early seventh. Eric Bloodaxe would have been quite at home with Ragnar 'Hairy-Breeches' and Ivar the Boneless in the middle of the ninth century; he was a jarring anachronism by the late 940s. The son of Athelstan's ally Harold 'Fairhair', who had died in 930, Eric had been thrown out of his own kingdom by the Norwegians; they preferred the milder rule of Eric's brother Hakon 'the Good' (who had been reared at Athelstan's court). When Eric turned up in northern England in late 947, the Northumbrian secession party headed by Archbishop Wulfstan immediately chose him as their new leader, only to realize what a mistake they had made. What they needed was a combined statesman, diplomat, law-giver and reliable national leader; what they got was an obsolete Viking warrior chief who proved hopelessly inadequate in all four roles.

Eadred was the king who decided that the time for the diplomatic handling of the Northumbrians was over. He resembled Alfred in that he, too, had grown to manhood and become king with the object-lessons of his brothers' reigns before his eyes. He dealt out savage punishment to the Northumbrians in 948, ravaging the entire country and not shrinking even from the destruction of the beautiful abbey church at Ripon. Enough Northumbrians nevertheless clung to Eric to enable a surprise attack to be made on Eadred's withdrawing army at Castleford, inflicting heavy casualties. The infuriated English king was prevented from marching back into Northumbria only by the hasty surrender of the rebel councillors who swore to abandon the fugitive Eric. So they did – only to elevate a new Norse king, Olaf Sihtricsson, in 949.

This seems to have left Eadred momentarily baffled. His position was not easy; faced with a rebel archbishop who had nevertheless received his *pallium* from the Pope in Rome, any Christian king would have been unsure of how far he could go. But when in 952 the Northumbrians expelled Sihtricsson and turned to Eric again, Eadred decided that enough was enough. He put Wulfstan in jail – presumably when the archbishop had come south, either on church business or to attend the Witan – and kept him there for the next two years. Eric remained, but he was now as much of an embarrassment to the Northumbrians as a problem for Eadred. Within two years Eric, a fugitive once more, was dead. Roger of Wendover says that he was 'treacherously killed by Earl Maccus in a certain lonely place which is called Stainmore, with his son Haeric and his brother Ragnald, betrayed by Earl Oswulf; and then afterwards King Eadred ruled in these districts.'

Eric Bloodaxe came to be remembered with all the affectionate nostalgia which Americans reserve for Billy the Kid and his ilk; he was the stuff of which sagas are made. For the English it seemed particularly appropriate that Eric met his end on Stainmore as a result of *Norse* treachery. It was the end of an era, and in more ways than one. Eric was the last of many Norse adventurers who had tried to conquer and hold Northumbria over the previous fifty years. But he was also, if only briefly and sporadically, the last independent king of York, where English kings had ruled for nearly 400 years. Simeon of Durham noted the formal passing of the last kingdom of the Anglo-Saxon heptarchy – Northumbria, once the greatest power in Britain: 'Here the kings of the Northumbrians came to an end, and henceforward the province was administered by earls.'

Above all, the death of Eric Bloodaxe ushered in a quarter-century of peace on which Saxon England was destined to look back as a golden age. For the first time since the early 830s, England was free of attack by foreign enemies. Eadred had brought the kingdom safely through the turbulent aftermath of the Reconquest; the last year of his life was taken up with the work of national reconstruction, including the release and restoration of Archbishop Wulfstan to his province in 954. Eadred himself died at Frome in Wessex on 23 November 955. He was remembered as an iron-fisted ruler who had slaughtered the people of Thetford in 952 for killing an abbot; but his will left lavish sums of money for the benefit of Church and people throughout England, with the pointed exception of Northumbria. He showed the cautious forethought of his father Edward in bequeathing a large sum of cash to be used for famine relief or, if necessary, to buy off an enemy army.

Like Athelstan, Eadred died childless and the line of succession passed to the teenage sons of Edmund: Eadwig, aged about fifteen, and Edgar, who was twelve. Eadwig was duly elected king, his youth enhancing the vital role of the Witan as a counselling body. Unfortunately Eadwig gave few signs of readiness to accept counsel from anybody. The clerical historians of his reign combine to give the young king an appalling press, branding him as a feckless and defiant juvenile who crossed his councillors like a naughty schoolboy. It all seems a little hard. Eadwig was, after all, the youngest new king in living or written memory, faced with no national peril, with all the good looks of his family (his popular name was Eadwig 'the All-Fair'), determined to have a good time – and probably heartily sick of being lectured about his revered ancestors. Given sympathetic coaching he would probably have grown out of it in no time, but all he got was a barrage of sanctimonious heckling from the clergy.

The young king was never allowed to forget that at his coronation feast he had slipped away to a private room to flirt with an opportunist lady with a royal marriage in mind – for herself or her daughter, who was also present. Despatched by Archbishop Oda, Abbot Dunstan and Bishop Cynesige caught Eadwig on a couch with the ladies, his crown lying abandoned on the floor. After berating the women for their 'folly', Dunstan dragged Eadwig away by main force, clapped the crown back on his head and hauled the protesting monarch back to his proper place at the high table in hall. Not surprisingly, the incident confirmed Eadwig's distaste for clergymen in general and Dunstan in particular. Dunstan's biographer tells how Eadwig subsequently deprived Dunstan of his property and forced the abbot to leave the country – but it does not add that Eadwig also married the girl, Aelfgifu, whom Dunstan had harangued that night. In retaliation, Archbishop Oda forced the royal couple to separate in 956 on grounds of consanguinity, that much-used instrument of medieval politics. Winchester, however, remembered Aelfgifu with gratitude for her gift of alms, among the other 'illustrious women' who had 'commended themselves to the prayers of the community'. Nor can it be said that Eadwig himself went so far as to sever the royal tradition of munificence to the Church; at least one charter has survived of a land grant by him to the archbishopric of York.

No excuses, however, can disguise the fact that Eadwig was simply incapable of ruling the kingdom created by his grandfather, father, and uncles. By 957 the Mercians and Northumbrians had had enough of Eadwig and chosen his younger brother Edgar to rule them instead, with the title 'King of the Mercians and Northumbrians and Britons'. A cynic will note that not one of Eadwig's pious critics, while approving the decision to divide the kingdom, paused to give thanks that no enemies were waiting in the wings to attack England, as had been the case only ten years before. The mind recoils from what might have been achieved by a Norse army led by a king who knew his business, striking at the boy kings' realms while they remained apart. Happily the danger did not exist, although Eadred had, as we have seen, provided for it in his will. In any event, this moment of great weakness for Saxon England was soon past. Eadwig died in Wessex on 1 October 959 and Edgar, now nearly sixteen years old, was accepted as king by the West Saxons.

Reunited, the kingdom of England now waited to see whether Edgar could put up a better performance as king than his late and generally unlamented brother. On the face of it, there were few omens to indicate that one of the most splendid reigns in English history had begun.

English fyrdmen, armed with axe and spear. During the long years of peace under Eadwig and Edgar, the military preparedness of the kingdom gradually slackened and decayed.

uni dequatos

RT Serto uterit n

DIES · XX

IVNI · 7

XIX   I P E IIII N̄   Inquadris col

VIII   C   Q G III   N̄   Coeabus ane

x consecrans uirgo scarque kalendas
narcellinusque perrusque.
xoenigen sociatur marchis.

6 Edgar 'the Peaceable' and Edward 'the Martyr' 959-978

As the conquered English writhed under the first Norman kings in the late eleventh century, the fifteen-year reign of Edgar 'the Peaceable', only a hundred years before, seemed to them to possess all the magic of legend. When Edgar was king England was rich, proud, and free, a land no foe in the world dared to attack. The great king had ruled his tranquil land with living saints as his councillors, and after his untimely death things had gone from bad to worse. For this reason, Edgar is the only English king in the *Anglo-Saxon Chronicle* to be honoured with a eulogy inserted at the outset as well as the close of his reign. After he had succeeded Eadwig in 959, the *Chronicle* recounts that in his days

> . . . things improved greatly, and God granted him that he lived in peace as long as he lived; and, as was necessary for him, he laboured zealously for this; he exalted God's praise far and wide, and loved God's law; and he improved the peace of the people more than the kings who were before him in the memory of man. And God also supported him so that kings and earls willingly submitted to him and were subjected to whatever he wished. And without battle he brought under his sway all that he wished. He came to be honoured widely throughout the countries, because he zealously honoured God's name, and time and again meditated on God's law, and exalted God's praise far and wide, and continually and frequently directed all his people wisely in matters of Church and State. . .

And when he died in 975, only thirty-two years old:

> In this year died Edgar, ruler of the Angles, friend of the West Saxons and protector of the Mercians. It was widely known throughout many nations across the gannet's bath, that kings honoured Edmund's son far and wide, and paid homage to this king as was his due by birth. Nor was there fleet so proud nor host so strong that it got itself prey in England as long as the noble king held the throne.

PREVIOUS PAGES English peasants reap a perfect harvest. After Edgar's death in 975 his reign was remembered as a golden age of peace, security and prosperity.

When all the eulogies are set aside, what remains? First and foremost, the truth behind the nickname: Edgar was a 'peaceable' king because nobody attacked him. Unlike nearly all his sorely-tried predecessors over the previous one hundred years, Edgar had the immense good fortune to reign at a time when the Scandinavian homeland was largely quiescent. One almost feels that a better soubriquet for Edgar would be 'the Lucky', if only for this reason. Searching the *Chronicle* for an impression of the overall history of Edgar's reign, it is hard to avoid the impression that the clerks were desperate for copy. Edgar becomes king in 959, recalls Dunstan and makes him bishop of Worcester, then London; in 961 the King promotes Dunstan to the archbishopric of Canterbury. At last, in 962, some news: Edgar's kinsman Aelfgar dies and is buried at Wilton. A mysterious King Sigeferth kills himself and is buried at Wimborne. There is 'a very great mortality' this year, and a 'great and fatal fire' in London – St Paul's Minster gets burned down, but is rebuilt the same year. Finally, Aethelmod the priest goes to Rome and dies there on 15 August. So it continues, year after year; all that is demanded of the King, it seems, is to appoint a new bishop now and again. For four of his fifteen years as king there are no entries at all.

This absence of man-made crises is, of course, a glowing testimonial to a solidly competent ruler. The king as good steward had been Alfred's ideal, from which (*see p. 62*) he had known himself to be sadly distracted by constant wars. It fell to Edgar to fulfil that ideal in conditions such as no king since Alfred, not even Athelstan, had enjoyed. The best administrators are not remembered for causing chaos and upheaval; they think ahead and nip potential trouble in the bud. When contrasted to the mistakes and follies committed by Eadwig which had literally divided the whole kingdom, Edgar's unexciting competence deserves all the praise which has ever been lavished on it. There is a very strong parallel between the lessons Alfred learned from the reigns of his father and brother Aethelbald, and the lessons Edgar learned from Eadwig. Both Alfred and Edgar had seen what happened when the rules of kingship were bent too far: their predecessors had not only rocked the ship of state, but had come close to sinking it. Like Alfred, Edgar settled down to rule his kingdom with his eyes and ears open.

When it came to the business of ruling England, Edgar was again immensely lucky. He had to repair the damage done by Eadwig, and he did not even have to find the men, lay or clerical, to help him do it. To administer the shires, the great and efficient ealdormen – Aelfhere of Mercia, Brihtnoth of Essex,

OVERLEAF King and Witan as the source of all justice – in the case of the felon on the gallows, short and sharp. The House of Lords is still the supreme law court of England.

ſteꝛ þ̃ am ᵹeꝛuꝛum pharao mæ
ꝇhꞇ hæꞇheꞇe ꞃaꝛeꞇan up oꝛþaꝛ

Aethelwold of East Anglia, Aelfheah of Hampshire – had all been appointed before Edgar's accession. To reform the English Church, and make its art, culture and learning the envy of the civilized world, Edgar merely had to appoint prelates of such eminence as Dunstan, Aethelwold and Oswald, whom he made respectively Archbishop of Canterbury, Bishop of Winchester, and Archbishop of York. (All three were subsequently venerated as saints.)

Edgar, then, must be credited with making the fullest use of the galaxy of talent placed at his disposal by his own appointments and those of his predecessors. In no sense can he be thought of as a 'rubber-stamp' king, mutely assenting to measures drawn up by his councillors and placed in front of him for his signature – the Old English Witan did not work that way. The king was the mainspring of the machine; his advisors advised.

It was in Edgar's reign that the law of the land was comprehensively revised to take account of the enormous changes in the land which had occurred since the days of Edward and Athelstan. One such measure may indeed have been taken by Edgar's predecessors (scholarly debate on whether or not this is the case seems likely to continue): this was the Hundred Ordinance, which defined the duties of the basic territorial unit of the kingdom. Each 'hundred' (building-block of the shire), was to have a 'moot' or court which assembled every four weeks and see to it that the king's law was obeyed: '. . . each man is to do justice to another'. The Hundred Ordinance was a highly important measure for the consolidation of local government on a national basis, for the Danelaw also had its hundreds, known as *wapentakes*.

With the Hundred Ordinance as a starting-point, Edgar's revised laws were drawn up 'to be common to all the nation, whether Englishmen, Danes or Britons, in every province of my dominion', and enforced through the boroughs (town) and hundreds or wapentakes (country):

> . . . it is my will that every man is to be under surety both within the boroughs and outside the boroughs.
>
> And witness is to be appointed for each borough and each hundred.

Dunstan ordering Edgar to lay aside his crown. The king's consecration, so long delayed, provided the foundation for the modern English coronation service.

Thirty-six are to be chosen as witness for each borough; twelve for small boroughs and for each hundred, unless you wish for more.

And every man is with their witness to buy and sell all goods that he buys and sells, in either a borough or a wapentake. . .

In other words, the law stated that the people of England must provide their own legal chaperones to ensure honest trading throughout the land. Edgar's laws are also remarkable for the formal grant of effective legal 'home rule' to the Danelaw:

Further, it is my will that there should be in force among the Danes such good laws as they best decide on, and I have ever allowed them this and will allow it so long as my life lasts, because of your loyalty, which you have always shown me. ...

If then my reeve or any other man, in high or low position, refuses it, and offers indignity either to the villagers or their herdsmen, the Danes are to decide by law what punishment they wish to apply in that matter.

The concluding paragraphs of the law code issued by Edgar at 'Wihtbordesstan', some time in 962–3, show a similar recognition of provincial independence elsewhere in the kingdom:

Among the English, I and my councillors have decided what the punishment shall be, if any man offers resistance or goes to the length of slaying any one of those who are concerned in this investigation and who inform about concealed cattle, or any of those who give true witness and by their truthfulness save the innocent and lawfully bring destruction upon the guilty.

It is, then, my will that what you have decided upon for the improvement of public order, with great wisdom and in a way very pleasing to me, shall be ever observed among you.

And this addition is to be common to all of us who inhabit these islands.

Now Earl Oslac and all the host who dwell in his aldermanry [York] are to give their support that this may be enforced, for the praise of God and the benefit of the souls of all of us and the security of all people.

And many documents are to be written concerning this, and sent both to Ealdorman Aelfhere [in Mercia] and Ealdorman Aethelwine [in East Anglia], and they are to send them in all directions, that this measure may be known to both the poor and the rich.

I will be a very gracious lord to you as long as my life lasts, and I am very well pleased with you all, because you are so zealous about the maintenance of the peace.

Edgar's performance as lawgiver received its highest praise half a century later, when Canute the Dane was beginning to rule an England conquered after two disastrous decades of war. 'It is my will', wrote Canute to his new subjects, 'that all the nation, ecclesiastical and lay, shall steadfastly observe Edgar's laws.' As Canute saw it, the trusted and familiar laws of Edgar were the best possible foundation for establishing a new and alien dynasty in England. No greater compliment could be paid

OPPOSITE Edgar, crowned at last, offers the charter for the New Minster at Winchester to Christ.

to Edgar and his legislation – his most impressive achievement. It was practical; and it endured.

The practical side of Edgar's reign is also shown by that other yardstick of Saxon royal administration: official charters. Those of Edgar are very different from the over-written effusions which had flattered Athelstan's vanity. Edgar's charters are short and crisp, usually a third of the length of Athelstan's and far more precise in the legal description of the property concerned. This may be attributed to the overhaul of clerical posts carried out by Edgar's zealous monastic bishops. The latter were not cloistered saints but shrewd and critical officials, dedicated to rooting out abuse in any form, including the slovenly offices of bureaucratic clerks who preferred showing off their Latin to expressing themselves clearly and concisely.

When he thought it necessary, Edgar was not afraid to show the mailed fist. For 969, the drowsy recital of ecclesiastical appointments in the *Chronicle* is punctuated by the startling entry: 'In this year King Edgar ordered all Thanet to be ravaged.' This was punishment on the Thanet islanders for having imprisoned and robbed Northumbrian merchants who had landed there. However, it was more than punishment; it was a political gesture of atonement, made for the benefit of the Northumbrians, and a public demonstration to all Edgar's subjects that the king's peace could not be broken with impunity.

One of the most important moments in Edgar's reign had a profound influence on the subsequent history of the English monarchy, namely his coronation. This, oddly enough, did not take place until 973, Edgar's thirtieth year, only two years before his death. The reason for the long delay was Dunstan's laborious revision of traditional coronation practices into a solemn new ceremony. To Dunstan the most sacred moment of the coronation was not the crowning itself but the anointing of the new king. This bore a direct relationship to the consecration of a priest. (The lowest age for canonical ordination into the priesthood, it must be noted, was also the candidate's thirtieth year.) A thousand years after Dunstan the solemnity of the anointing is still preserved in the modern English coronation service.

The coronation took place at Bath, on Whit Sunday 973, and

OPPOSITE Edgar enthroned, wearing the distinctive four-square crown designed – as with every other detail of the coronation and its regalia – by Dunstan.

Corfe Castle: a picturesque ruin today but a place of horror to English minds a thousand years ago, when Edward 'the Martyr' was murdered there.

Pictura et scriptura huius pagine subtus
uisa est de propria manu sci dunstani.
Tho: Alley D.D.
NE. D.2.19.
(2176)
Bod. 578.
Uirga recta est
Uenite filii audite me timore dni docebo uos
Uirga regni tui.
Dunstanum memet clemens rogo xpe tuere
Tenarias me non si
sorbsisse procellas

was followed by the most celebrated incident connected with Edgar: his voyage to Chester with his fleet to receive the six (or eight, depending on which source is preferred) British client-kings. After formally renewing their homage to the newly-crowned King of the English, the British rulers are said to have rowed him from his palace to the church of St John on the River Dee, while he steered. The essential point about the incident is that the British kings' homage was voluntary, unprompted by any recent defeat at the hands of the English, but extending a tradition begun in the reigns of Athelstan and Edmund.

ABOVE Preferment from the King: a new bishop is appointed and installed.

OPPOSITE St Dunstan, Edgar's foremost adviser, prostrates himself at the feet of Christ.

127

Royal passenger, royal
crew: the sub-kings of
Celtic Britain row Edgar
on the Dee in homage.

Two years later, on 8 July 975, Edgar died suddenly with his
last important duty still unfulfilled. He had not lived long
enough for his sons to reach manhood. Edward, the son of
Edgar's first marriage, was about fifteen; Ethelred, son of the
King's second marriage to Aelfthryth (widow of Ealdorman
Aethelwold of East Anglia) was barely ten. Thus the two
athelings were even younger than Eadwig and Edgar had been
when Eadred died in 955, and unpleasant memories of Eadwig
were naturally aroused. To some, however, the prospect of a
minor succeeding was not wholly unwelcome. These were a
group of ealdormen, headed by Aelfhere of Mercia, who had
become increasingly restive at Edgar's constant deeding of land
to the monasteries, a process which, if continued indefinitely,
would make the abbots of the Church the predominant
landowners in the shires. As Dunstan supported the claim of
Edward, the eldest atheling, there seemed little doubt that the
Archbishop would prevail on Edward, if elected, to maintain
his father's policies. The anti-monastic faction therefore began
to press for the succession of Ethelred; but when the Witan met

for the election Dunstan, his bishops, and the loyal ealdormen –
Brihtnoth of Essex foremost among the latter – secured the
throne for Edward.

The only pen portrait we have of Edward is not an attractive
one. According to the anonymous biographer of St Oswald of
York, Edward 'inspired in all not only fear but even terror, for
[he scourged them?] not only with words but truly with blows,
and especially his own men dwelling with him.' The prospect of
a violent, tantrum-throwing, pro-monastic teenager as king
can certainly not have been less irksome than the notorious
fecklessness of Eadwig twenty years before.

The brief reign of Edward II (as he should, in theory, be
styled) is gloomily recorded as a time of worsening troubles
predicted by the appearance of a comet in the year of his
accession, and begun in 976 with a famine. Although Dunstan
and his colleagues strove to hold their ground in the Witan as
best they could, the *Chronicle* records that Aelfhere and the anti-
monastic party came out into the open soon after Edward's
accession:

> In his days because of his youth, the adversaries of God, Ealdorman
> Aelfhere and many others, broke God's law and hindered the
> monastic life, and destroyed monasteries and dispersed the monks
> and put to flight the servants of God, whom King Edgar had
> ordered the holy Bishop Aethelwold to institute; and they
> plundered widows time and again.

'And many wrongs and evil lawless acts rose up afterwards,'
concludes this woeful if somewhat breathless passage, 'and ever
after that it grew much worse.'

'Much worse' is putting it mildly; the upshot was a plot to
assassinate Edward. According to St Oswald's biographer, the
main conspirators were the 'zealous thanes' in the service of the
atheling Ethelred. But these thanes were only the executioners;
it is hard to believe that Aelfhere, and Ethelred's mother
Aelfthryth, were not closely involved. The murder must have
taken considerable planning in order to make sure of catching
Edward off guard, without his own escort. The plotters finally
struck on 18 March 978, at Corfe Gap, where Ethelred was
staying with his mother and where Edward rode to the hall to
greet his brother and stepmother, unsuspecting and unescorted.

The scene as described by St Oswald's biographer is unbearably vivid. First the sighting of the King's horse approaching the hill on which Corfe Castle stands today. Then Aelfthryth and Ethelred, coming out at the head of their retinue to greet Edward as he rode up the hill in the late afternoon light; the cupbearer stepping forward to offer Edward the stirrup-cup and the armed thanes moving in as if to help the king dismount, closing round his horse:

> ... the thanes then holding him, one drew him on the right towards him as if he wished to give him a kiss, but another seized roughly his left hand and also wounded him. And he shouted, so far as he could: 'What are you doing – breaking my right arm?' And suddenly leapt from his horse and died.

Edward 'The Martyr', as he was soon to be revered, was not the first king to be murdered in England, with or without treachery; but his murder horrified the nation with its cold-blooded overtones. Implicated among the guilty parties were the dead king's brother, stepmother, and servants; and nobody, not even one of the thanes, was ever punished for the crime. 'And no worse deed than this for the English people was committed since first they came to Britain,' is the *Chronicle*'s famous comment before recording how 'very quickly after that', Ethelred was consecrated at Kingston.

OPPOSITE Romantic print of Edward's murder at Corfe. As the King takes the stirrup-cup from Aelfthryth on his arrival, an armed thane steals behind him to strike the King down.

dedmund
frcū laē

7

im eleuat. enſem nibc. nauta uehemena incaſ

Cnuto rex dace.

Daci

Æthelred 'Evil-Counsel'
and Edmund 'Ironside'
978-1016

WHETHER WE ADMIT it or not, we all tend to judge historic monarchs and their reigns by the old schoolroom quartet of values: Good or Bad, Strong or Weak. In the case of Ethelred of England the choice is halved: Bad or Weak. He was the least effective of the Saxon kings and, unhappily for his people, the one with the longest reign; he inevitably became the Saxon king whom posterity has saddled with the most opprobrious reputation, the first in a category of medieval English kings whose reigns are best remembered for their negative values: Stephen, John, Edward II, Henry VI. In 978 Ethelred became king of a rich, powerful and renowned country; when he died thirty-eight years later he left it humiliated, prostrate, overrun with enemy forces and on the brink of total defeat. It had taken a lot of doing.

The most surprising feature of Ethelred's reign is that it lasted so long. Saxon England had always been a rough school for incompetent rulers, who tended to meet early and violent deaths or, if lucky, expulsion and exile. But as long as he lived the English were extraordinarily loyal to Ethelred, and this is a point in his favour which is usually forgotten. His notorious nickname 'Ethelred the Unready' was coined centuries after his death and is mistaken. 'Ethelred' means 'noble counsel' and adding *unred*, signifying an act of crime or treason, was a cynical thirteenth-century pun to suggest that his name should have been 'evil counsel'. Even that, however, is not wholly appropriate. Kings, like electorates, get the politicians they deserve, but the councillors of the Witan under Ethelred never took the obvious step of ousting their useless monarch and electing a proper leader. When Ethelred did go into brief exile in 1013 the Witan coaxed him back at the earliest opportunity with one of the biggest compliments ever paid to an incompetent ruler: the assurance 'that no lord was dearer to them than their natural lord, if he would govern them more justly than before'. And here, even in the closing years of his life and disastrous reign, is the biggest clue to the historic Ethelred: the determined and even passionate feeling that England's troubles were not really the King's fault, and that he must be given yet another chance.

Certainly Ethelred himself could never forget that he had become king as the result of the worst crime in his country's

PREVIOUS PAGES Duel of the giants: Edmund 'Ironside' and Canute, fancifully depicted in personal combat, struggle for the mastery of England.

history, his own brother Edward being struck down before his eyes so that he, Ethelred, could step into his place. Ethelred was a frightened boy at the moment of the murder at Corfe; he grew into a guilty and insecure man, quick to appease and offer compensation. No one blamed him for this because it was a guilty and insecure age. The millennium was coming and with it, perhaps, the end of the world. As the Church taught, this would be preceded by a darkening age of natural disasters, crime, war and treachery on earth – 'brother against brother'. The violence of the anti-monastic faction in England, the appalling murder of King Edward, the mounting tempo of Viking attacks which once again began to afflict the English within a couple of years of Ethelred's accession – it all seemed to fit. Even for those who managed to control their religious apprehensions and look at the world as it was, a feeling that Ethelred must be supported until he was old enough to govern properly nevertheless reflected this national guilt complex. Given the opportunity, the King might make everything all right again.

This tremulous hope for a fresh start explains the slightly hysterical rejoicing at Ethelred's accession mentioned in the *Chronicle*. It was echoed by St Oswald's biographer, who makes the interesting point that at least the new king looked the part:

> King Ethelred, the illustrious atheling, was consecrated to the supreme dignity of the kingdom by the apostolic man Dunstan and his co-apostle Oswald, and there was great rejoicing at his consecration. For he was young in years, graceful in manners, beautiful in face and comely in appearance. Soon indeed, before he had passed the age of adolescence, the Prince Behemoth rose against him, with all his preparation and his satellites, having with him *caelethi*, that is, slayers. During his reign the abominable Danes came to the kingdom of the English, and laying waste and burning everything, did not spare men ...

However, the first two years of Ethelred's reign passed very quietly; it is noticeable that the chroniclers' lamentations over the persecution of the monasteries cease with Ethelred's coronation. Aelfhere of Mercia was now the leading secular power in the land and it was he – not Ethelred, or even Archbishop Dunstan – who presided over what amounted to a ceremony of national atonement in March 979, on the first anniversary of Edward's murder. The late king's body was exhumed from the undistinguished grave in Wareham where it had been laid to rest. It was found to be free of decay, a phenomenon then held to be a mark of divine favour and qualification for saintly honours. After a splendid funeral Edward's remains were reverently laid to rest in the nunnery at Shaftesbury, 'where Masses and sacred oblations were celebrated for the redemption of his soul', comments St Oswald's biographer, 'by the ealdorman's orders'.

The muted tranquillity of Ethelred's first two years was only the lull before the storm. From 980 Viking attacks on England suddenly began again; first raids of plunder, but very soon expeditions by full-scale armies exploiting the fact that England had changed. After twenty-five years of peace and prosperity the country was not only immensely rich in ready cash and treasure, it had a feeble young king with advisors who would

Feasting in hall. While his people suffered, Ethelred went through the motions of ruling from his luxurious court, where treachery and corruption flourished.

rather pay protection-money than fight. Once that vital intelligence had begun to circulate in Scandinavia, it was like the California gold rush. Any warrior chief, east of the North Sea or in the Norse colonies in Ireland, could easily fit out and man a raiding fleet once he announced that the target was England. And the damage was done in the first ten years of Ethelred's reign, when the first raiders returned to port laden with plunder instead of ruefully counting their casualties, vowing 'never again', and advising all interested parties to leave the English severely alone.

Even if Ethelred had been old enough to lead the army of England when the raids began in the early 980s, no one could have blamed him for failing to annihilate the first raiders. With the entire coastline of England open to them, they could hit and run as they chose and the only real chance of intercepting them was at sea, with an alert and sizeable navy. But the splendid fleet

RIGHT Shipbuilding, by royal command – but all Ethelred's efforts to recreate England's former prowess at sea came to nothing.

BELOW Stone memorial to the might of the Danes on land and sea.

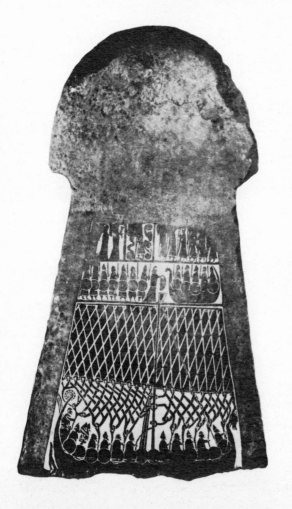

which had supported Athelstan's drive into Scotland forty-five years before, and which had been maintained even under Edgar, had been disbanded and laid up to save money – the very money which was luring the raiders to England. This left the raiders with a free hand at sea, and put the onus on the provincial ealdormen to engage the enemy when he actually came within reach on shore. During the first eight years of the renewed Viking attacks on England, however, not one raiding force was even intercepted, let alone destroyed to serve as a deterrent to others.

The raiders' impunity was certainly not due to their choosing targets in inaccessible regions, making it impossible for the English to get at them before they re-embarked. In 980, for instance, seven ships sacked Southampton; another force plundered the Isle of Thanet; while a third ravaged Cheshire. It was not Ethelred's fault that his ealdormen failed to wipe out these enemies: most of his ealdormen were old enough to remember the wars of Eadred. The real trouble seems to have been that they were not only out of practice after too long a

BELOW The north Somerset coast, where Ethelred's fyrdmen were shattered by a raiding fleet in 988.

period of peace; they were also too old. Most of the leading councillors of Edgar, in fact, died during Ethelred's first ten years: Aelthelmaer of Hampshire and Edwin of Sussex in 982; Aelfhere of Mercia in 983; Bishop Aethelwold in 984; and Archbishop Dunstan in 988. Just when Ethelred was reaching the age at which he would be expected to lead the country against its enemies, he was becoming increasingly deprived of seasoned fighting men and experienced councillors when he needed them most.

Ethelred's first recorded piece of statecraft, executed in 986 when he was twenty-one, was hardly encouraging, although there were precedents for it. Giving no reasons for the act, the *Chronicle* records that 'the King laid waste the diocese of Rochester'. Though there is no mention of any Viking attack in this year, a likely explanation is that the Kentishmen of the Medway refused to do their duty when faced with an unrecorded attack, and that Ethelred decided to make an example of them – as his father had done with the Thanet islanders in 969 – *pour encourager les autres*. Two years later, when a Viking fleet swept down on the Somersetshire coastal town of Watchet and razed it, the local fyrd did march out and fight, and were soundly beaten. Snatching at straws, writers like St Oswald's biographer stoutly affirmed that the English had won all the glory:

> A very severe battle took place in the west, in which our countrymen, who are called Devonshiremen, strongly resisted and obtained the victory of a holy triumph, thus gaining glory. Many of our side fell, more of theirs. For of our men, a most brave thane, Streonwold by name [the *Chronicle* gives this worthy's name as Goda], was killed with some others, who preferred to end their lives by a warlike death than to live in shame.

It was still a defeat, nevertheless, and posthumous glory was no substitute for victory.

The next defeat, three years later, was even worse, though it went straight into legend and became the subject of an epic poem: the battle of Maldon, surpassed only by Brunanburh as the most famous battle in the history of Saxon England. It was fought and lost against a fleet of ninety-three ships commanded by Olaf Tryggvason (afterwards King of Norway), which ravaged from the North Foreland all the way round the Thames

Estuary and up the east coast to Ipswich. At Maldon, however, the veteran Ealdorman Brihtnoth with the fyrd of Essex trapped Olaf's men on a tidal islet, and then – as the poem has it – chivalrously yielded his advantage to allow a fairly matched engagement to be fought on dry land. The Essex men, including Brihtnoth, were wiped out; but the English were immensely proud of the way Brihtnoth's companions stood and died to the last man rather than survive their fallen lord. There was a significant tendency to forget that this was not how Alfred had saved Wessex one hundred years before.

All the heroism of Maldon was then jeopardized when Archbishop Sigeric advised Ethelred to buy off Olaf's fleet. This was the cue for Ethelred to show his quality, reject the advice with maximum publicity and take the field at the head of the English army in the south-east. Instead he took the Archbishop's advice and opened negotiations with Olaf. The subsequent truce was solemnized in a formal treaty which bore the sorriest comparison with Alfred's treaty with Guthrum. For all the clauses about equal status and future immunity for English merchant shipping, this was a barefaced piece of appeasement, granting the raiders indemnity from payment for the damage they had done and agreeing to pay a monstrous Danegeld of 22,000 pounds in gold and silver. It was one of the biggest mistakes Ethelred ever made.

As far as the *Chronicle* is concerned, the treaty of 991 is the prologue to an appalling story of incompetence, treachery and defeat, growing increasingly worse over the last twenty-five years of Ethelred's reign. In their length and wealth of detail, the *Chronicle*'s entries from 991 to 1016 are the most informative since the last wars of Alfred and the years of the Reconquest under Edward and Aethelflaed; but Ethelred's wars hardly bear comparison with those of Alfred and Edward. The chroniclers who recorded these bitter years did not shrink from severe criticism of the failure to wage effective war against the national enemy. It was not criticism aimed at Ethelred, however; the phrase invariably used is 'the King and his councillors'. In its coverage of England's ordeal at the hands of the Danes under Ethelred, the *Chronicle* conveys vividly a sense of frustrated but unshakeable patriotism, lambasting a useless government but never going so far as to attack the king in person for refusing to

England's fate under the unwarlike leadership of Ethelred: not victory in battle, but humiliation by Danegeld.

lead the army, or for continuing to trust proven traitors, or for alienating important allies by acts of spite and cruelty – in short, for being the worst war-leader in the history of Saxon England.

One example will suffice to illustrate this frustration – the *Chronicle* entry for 999:

> In this year the army came again [from the Isle of Wight] round into the Thames and turned then up the Medway and to Rochester. And the Kentish levy came against them there, and they then joined battle stoutly; but, alas! they too soon turned and fled because they had not the support which they should have had, and the Danes had control of the field. And they then seized horses and rode wherever they pleased, and destroyed and ravaged almost all West Kent. Then the king with his councillors determined that they should be opposed by a naval force and also by a land force. But when the ships were ready, one delayed from day to day, and oppressed the wretched people who were on the ships. And ever, as things should have been moving, they were the more delayed from one hour to the next, and ever they let their enemies' force increase,

and ever the English retreated inland and the Danes continually followed; and then in the end it effected nothing – the naval expedition or the land expedition – except the oppression of the people and the waste of money and the encouragement of their enemies.

In addition to his private fears and uncertainties, Ethelred shrank from commanding his forces in person, a duty performed as a matter of course by every previous king of England and the kingdoms of the heptarchy. He is on record as having taken the field only three times in his thirty-eight-year reign: in 1000, 1009 and 1014. On none of these occasions did he accomplish anything of strategic value, let alone bring the Danes to battle. In 1000, while the raiding fleet had crossed to Normandy for the summer, Ethelred led an expedition to ravage Strathclyde while his fleet harried the Norse colony on the Isle of Man. In 1009 Ethelred actually intercepted the Danish army as it withdrew to its ships, laden with 3,000 pounds extorted from the people of east Kent and the spoils of Sussex, Hampshire and Berkshire. The English army was burning to attack but Ethelred was successfully dissuaded by Eadric, Ealdorman of Mercia, whose double-dealing made him the most hated man in England. And Ethelred's last expedition, in 1014, was a brutal punitive expedition against the people of the Danelaw because they had yielded to the Danish King Sweyn for want of English support.

There is not a shred of evidence to suggest that Ethelred's position as king was ever jeopardized because he was not a royal war-leader in the traditional mould. What people found intolerable was his failure to appoint loyal and competent commanders to do the fighting for him. The Ealdorman Aelfric of Mercia had been exiled from the land for some unknown crime in 985, but by 992 Ethelred had reinstated him. In that year Aelfric was made one of the four commanders (two of them bishops) appointed 'to try if they could entrap the Danish army anywhere at sea'. Aelfric, however, betrayed the English plans to the enemy who escaped, then he abandoned his command and fled. Ethelred's reaction, typically spiteful, was to have his son blinded in the following year, but by 1003 Aelfric was back in command of the English army, 'up to his old tricks' as the *Chronicle* scathingly records. Having located the

Danish army raiding that year, 'as soon as they were so close that each army looked on the other, he feigned him sick, and began retching to vomit, and said that he was taken ill, and thus betrayed the people whom he should have led.'

It took another four years before Ethelred replaced Aelfric, but the new ealdorman of Mercia was even worse: Eadric Streona, a ruthless turncoat whose skill at exploiting his importance to both sides was unequalled until the career of Warwick the Kingmaker in the Wars of the Roses, 450 years later. For ten years Eadric's trimming and treachery enabled him to flourish under two successive English kings (Ethelred and his son Edmund) and their Danish enemies (Sweyn and his son Canute).

Ethelred's adherence to treacherous subordinates was bad enough, but his lunatic policy towards the Danish population of England was fatal. Failing to see that the staunch loyalty of the Danelaw was one of the biggest assets he had, Ethelred's fearful distrust of the Danish population as potential fifth-columnists led him into the cardinal error of his reign. In 1001 Earl Pallig, apparently disgusted with Ethelred's inability to defend his lands, defected to Sweyn 'with the ships that he could collect'. Pallig's defection seems to have been the trigger for Ethelred's order of a widespread, and hence carefully prepared, massacre of Danes throughout England – the 'St Brice's Day Massacre' of 13 November 1002. There is a sickeningly hypocritical note of self-justification in a charter granted to St Frideswide's monastery in Oxford, two years later, a typical example of Ethelred's furtive propaganda in defence of his own misrule:

> ... I will relate in a few words to all who look upon this document for what reason it was done. For it is fully agreed that to all dwelling in this country it will be well known that, since a decree was sent out by me with the counsel of my leading men and magnates, to the effect that all the Danes who had sprung up in this island, sprouting like cockle amongst the wheat, were to be destroyed by a most just extermination, and this decree was to be put into effect even as far as death, those Danes who dwelt in [Oxford], striving to escape death, entered this sanctuary of Christ, having broken by force the doors and bolts, and resolved to make a refuge and defence for themselves therein against the people of the town and the suburbs; but when all the people in pursuit strove,

forced by necessity, to drive them out, and could not, they set fire to the planks and burnt, as it seems, this church with its ornaments and its books. Afterwards, with God's aid, it was renewed by me and my subjects, and, as I have said above, strengthened in Christ's name with the honour of a fresh privilege, along with the territories belonging to it, and endowed with every liberty, regarding royal exactions as well as ecclesiastical dues.

This bland statement of how desperate men and women were burned alive in a church to which they had fled for sanctuary is as callous and repellent as Cromwell's letter to Parliament describing how the Irishmen of Drogheda were burned alive in *their* churches. In Ireland the butchery of Drogheda is still vividly remembered today, after three centuries and more; the impact of the St Brice's Day Massacre on the Scandinavian world is easy to imagine. But the supreme folly was that the massacre's victims included Gunnhild, the sister of Sweyn of Denmark. This created a merciless blood-feud against the English which the Danish ruler never abated, proceeding from the widespread punishment of the English land to its conquest.

It should be noted that the abominable cowardice of the St Brice's Day Massacre closed a year which had opened with another massive payment of 24,000 pounds to the marauding Danish army. The massacre did nothing to lift the shadows from Ethelred's reputation and must have been a horrific introduction to England for Ethelred's second queen, Emma, daughter of Richard I, Duke of Normandy, who married Ethelred in the spring of 1002. By his first wife, Elgiva, Ethelred already had three sons. Two of these athelings had been named after their mighty forbears, Athelstan and Edmund – a fact which, in view of their father's dismal record as king, must have been the subject of much tart comment and hopeless nostalgia. The youngest atheling, less felicitously, had been named Eadwig.

Ethelred and Emma (whom the English knew by the Saxon name of Aelfgifu) had two sons of their own, who were also given illustrious names: Alfred and Edward. Unlike their half-brothers, who had been brought up in England by foster-mothers and the dowager queen Aelfthryth, Alfred and Edward were reared across the Channel in their mother's country as Norman princes. Thus the marriage between

145

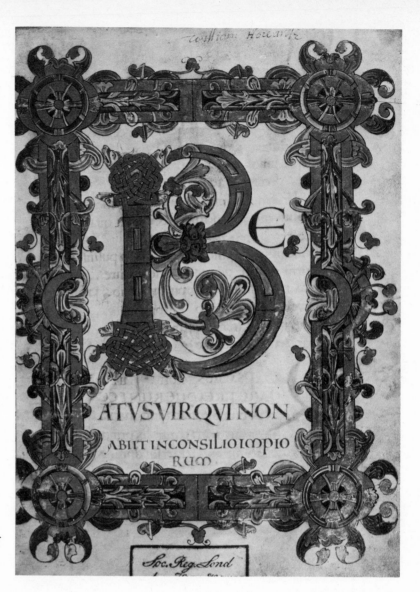

The 'Beatus page' from an Anglo-Saxon psalter of the early eleventh century.

Ethelred and Emma in 1002 established the fateful dynastic link between England and Normandy which resulted, sixty-four years later, in the invasion of England by Ethelred's great-nephew by marriage – William of Normandy.

It took Sweyn of Denmark ten years to conquer England from Ethelred – rather less than the time it had taken Edward the Elder to reconquer East Anglia and Danish Mercia nearly a century earlier. Before 1002 Sweyn learned little more than the obvious fact that Ethelred's England had become the most profitable country in Europe for plundering expeditions. Between 1002 and 1009 he learned much more: that Danish armies could march the length and breadth of England without serious molestation, extorting not merely tribute but transport and supplies from the helpless population. Finally, in 1009, Sweyn launched his biggest army yet against England, and this army had come to stay. It shattered what was left of the cohesion of the English kingdom after two decades of constant humiliation. 'Finally there was no leader who would collect an army, but each fled as best he could, and in the end no shire would even help the other,' laments the *Chronicle* for 1010. In the following year, after listing the piecemeal submission of the provinces to the Danish army, the *Chronicle* erupts in helpless rage. 'All these disasters befell us through bad policy, in that they were never offered tribute in time nor fought against; but when they had done most to our injury, peace and truce were made with them; and for all this truce and tribute they journeyed nonetheless in bands everywhere, and harried our wretched people, and plundered and killed them.'

With his country burning, his people dying, and his enemies destroying the fabric of his kingdom around him, Ethelred continued to go through the motions of ruling. The Witan met; grandiose defence measures were agreed and never implemented; charters were drawn up and witnessed; and revision after revision was made to the law of the land, urging the English to loyalty, obedience, and religious atonement for their obvious sins. In 1008 a revised law code formally recognized the late King Edward as a saint and fixed his saint's day as the anniversary of his murder: 18 March. 'Let us loyally support one royal lord,' the 1008 code concluded, 'and all together defend our lives and our land, as well as ever we can, and pray Almighty God from our inmost heart for his help.' But an emergency edict in the following year, prompted by the descent of the Danish army of 1009, began by putting the entire nation on a three-day fast of bread, water and herbs as a penance, and ended despairingly 'God help us. Amen'.

Though starved of any effective leadership by their king, the English resisted where they could, proving that Brihtnoth's example at Maldon had not been entirely in vain. In 1004 Ealdorman Ulfcetel and the East Anglians came close to trapping the entire Danish army, but the men sent to burn the Danish fleet failed to carry out their orders. The Danes brought

Ulfcetel's outnumbered force to action and finally destroyed it after a terrific battle; '... but if their full strength had been there', comments the *Chronicle*, 'the Danes would never have got back to their ships; as they themselves said, they never met worse fighting in England than Ulfcetel dealt to them.' (Ulfcetel had the great good sense to realize that a lost battle did not mean a lost war, and refused to die on the field; he led the East Anglians into action again in 1010, but this time his men broke and fled at the first shock.) And London, which had already beaten off an attack by Sweyn in 994, stood like a rock against the army of 1009. 'Praise be to God, it still stands untouched', exults the *Chronicle* for 1009, 'and they always suffered loss there.'

London was still holding out as Ethelred's last refuge two years later, when the Danes captured Archbishop Aelfheah of Canterbury and demanded an extra ransom for him. When Aelfheah bravely refused to ask his people for more sacrifices on his behalf the Danes pelted him unconscious with beef-bones

Archbishop Aelfheah defies his Danish captors by refusing to comply with their ransom demands. Martyrdom and sainthood were his reward.

from their feasting, finally smashing his head in with an axe. Even this was not the crowning ignominy for Ethelred. In 1013 the army of Sweyn headed north and overran the Danelaw, the bulk of which had remained loyal to Ethelred even after the St Brice's Day Massacre. But the submission of the Danelaw to Sweyn in 1013 marked the beginning of the end. The ealdormen and thanes of the western shires followed suit, and Sweyn's triumph was complete: '. . . all the nation regarded him as full king'. Then, and only then, the Londoners bowed to the inevitable and submitted to Sweyn in turn. By the new year of 1014 Ethelred had followed Emma, Alfred and Edward to exile in Normandy, leaving his tormented people under Danish rule.

A major mystery amid these tremendous events is the whereabouts of the elder athelings: Athelstan, Edmund and Eadwig. There is no suggestion that they joined their father, stepmother and half-brothers in Normandy. Their prospects of survival, with Eadric Streona ready to hunt them down and kill them in order to ingratiate himself with his new Danish master, were slim. However, Sweyn was only King of the English for a matter of weeks; he died on 3 February 1014. The Danish fleet in the Thames elected Sweyn's son Canute as their new king, but the English Witan had other ideas. Its councillors unanimously decided to recall Ethelred from Normandy, and sent their fugitive king the splendid message quoted above (*p. 134*). Ethelred reacted to this supreme opportunity with his personal brand of furtive caution, staying in Normandy himself but readily exposing his young son to whatever new treachery might be afoot in England:

> The King sent his son Edward hither with his messengers, and said that he would be a gracious lord to them, and reform all the things which they all hated; and all the things that had been said and done against him should be forgiven, on condition that they all unanimously turned to him without treachery. And complete friendship was then established with oath and pledge on both sides, and they pronounced every Danish king an outlaw from England for ever. Then during the spring King Ethelred came home to his own people and he was gladly received by them all.

Ethelred's return was followed by the rarest of phenomena – his taking command of the army for a military expedition. The

objective was the destruction of Canute and his army in the northern Danelaw, and for once Ethelred seems to have acted with commendable energy and speed. He advanced so fast that Canute was forced to take to his ships. Finding no Danes to fight, Ethelred then let loose the English army to burn and ravage the Danelaw province of Lindsey which had harboured Canute. Canute riposted by sailing south and landing the hostages who had been surrendered to his father at Sandwich – minus their ears, noses and hands. He then returned to Denmark, leaving Ethelred temporarily unchallenged in his restored kingdom.

The year 1015 saw the atheling Edmund emerge as the real leader of the English, challenging his father's authority and declaring himself champion of the Danelaw. Eadric of Mercia predictably turned coat again and declared for Ethelred, ingratiating himself with the King by treacherously killing the leading thanes of the Danelaw: Sigeferth and Morcar. Ethelred then seized all the property of the murdered thanes and ordered Sigeferth's widow Aldgyth to be brought to Malmesbury, presumably as a hostage to be used to keep the Danelaw quiescent. Edmund, however, took charge of Aldgyth himself; he carried her off and married her, then brought her home to the land of the Five Boroughs and took charge of all the estates of Sigeferth and Morcar. Thus, presented with an English champion of their interests for the first time in thirty-seven years, the people of the Five Boroughs enthusiastically accepted Edmund as their lord.

By the late summer of 1015, when Canute returned with a reinforced Danish army, all the hopes of the English for a genuine national recovery rested on Edmund. Ethelred was ill; the atheling Athelstan (whose will, bequeathing property to Sigeferth and Morcar as well as his father and brother, has survived) was already dead. Eadric of Mercia now represented a piece on the chess-board which neither Edmund nor Canute dared allow to remain 'loose'. Ostensibly honouring his allegiance to Ethelred, Eadric marched the Mercian army to join Edmund's against Canute, but Edmund hesitated to join forces and lay himself open to Eadric's notorious gambit – betrayal at the earliest favourable moment. Thus exposed by the atheling's obvious distrust, Eadric won over the crews of forty

OPPOSITE Particularly valuable for its wealth of costume detail, this illustration from the early eleventh century shows an English king demonstrating his prowess as a harpist.

ships and deserted to Canute, hopelessly isolating Wessex from Edmund and his scanty forces far away to the north-east. For the winter of 1015–16 the West Saxons prudently yielded to Canute and paid tribute.

All these preliminary moves set the scene for the tremendous campaign of 1016, a year, like 871, 877–8 and 917, when the qualities of royal leadership in England were tested to breaking-point. The spotlight rested on Edmund's efforts to raise a national army with which to fight Canute and Eadric. His first efforts were frustrated by the popular clamour for Ethelred to join the English army with the redoutable defenders of London, but the ailing king lent a ready ear to the rumours of treachery which his courtiers continually fed him, and stayed in London. Edmund next tried to make certain of Earl Uhtred of Northumbria, but Canute forestalled him by making a lightning march into Northumbria and browbeating Uhtred into submission. Canute then had Uhtred killed and replaced with his own nominee, Eric.

By April 1016 Canute's position was looking overwhelmingly strong. The Danish fleet at Southampton dominated the entire south coast; Canute was master of the Danelaw and Northumbria. Edmund, however, took the next trick, and a vital one, by making sure of London when Ethelred died on 23 April. The *Chronicle* spares him a brief, straight-faced epitaph: '... and he had held the kingdom with great toils and difficulties while his life lasted.' This is in deliberate contrast to the following sentence: 'And then after his death, all the councillors who were in London and the citizens chose Edmund as king, and he stoutly defended his kingdom while his life lasted.'

However, Edmund was accepted as king only in London; a much larger and admittedly more representative Witan, convened in Southampton, declared for Canute. After leaving London ready to face the inevitable attack by Canute, Edmund's first task was to head west and win the allegiance of the vital heartland of the kingdom: Wessex. As Canute and the Danes headed east to besiege London at the moment that Edmund began his tour of the west, the people of Wessex had no inhibitions in delightedly rallying to the resolute young King who seemed bent on surpassing the achievements of his historic namesake.

Throughout the summer of 1016 the fate of England turned on the defence of London, which held out as valiantly as ever and repelled all Canute's attacks. Edmund meanwhile, with the army of Wessex and the south, launched a series of spoiling attacks to crack the siege, counter-attacking first on the north bank of the Thames, then on the south. For their part the Danes, once committed to besieging London, were soon obliged to raid for provisions in Essex and Kent. After Edmund broke one of their divisions at Otford in Kent, chasing the survivors into the Isle of Sheppey, Eadric of Mercia changed sides again. With hindsight, the *Chronicle* agonizes over Edmund's mistaken decision to accept Eadric's allegiance: '. . . no greater folly was ever agreed to than that was.' From Edmund's point of view it was a calculated risk. Eadric's latest defection might well encourage others at a time when Edmund and his army needed every man they could get; and it would certainly dislocate Canute's plans. That such a dyed-in-the-wool turncoat as Eadric should choose this particular moment again to back the English cause was a propaganda victory not to be turned down.

Openwork silver disc, with a hawk grappling its prey at centre and the name 'Aelfgifu' round the rim. It has been suggested that this ornament may have belonged to Emma, queen of Ethelred and Canute, whose English name was Aelfgifu.

Unhappily the chronicler was right. At Ashingdon in Essex the armies of Wessex, Mercia and the south squared up for what Edmund intended to be the decisive battle with Canute on 18 October 1016. Timing his moment with the skill of long practice, Eadric deserted the English army as battle was joined. Edmund's men fought valiantly, but suffered a crushing defeat. 'There Canute had the victory', mourned the *Chronicle*, 'and won for himself all the English people. There was Bishop Eadnoth [of Dorchester] killed, and Abbot Wulfsige [of Ramsey], and Ealdorman Aelfric [of Hampshire], and Godwine, the ealdorman of Lindsey, and Ulfcetel of East Anglia, and Aethelweard, son of Ealdorman Aethelwine, and all the nobility of England was there destroyed.'

Edmund's reaction to the disaster at Ashingdon earned him the deathless title of 'Ironside' from his people. Just as Alfred the Great had done after his shattering midwinter defeat by Guthrum, Edmund fled far into the west, and began to raise yet another army. In his refusal to abandon the struggle after the Ashingdon débâcle, Edmund was acting as nothing less than the apparent reincarnation of Alfred the Great – a contrast to his father so great as to seem almost miraculous. It appears to have

153

Feeble father, valiant son: Ethelred (LEFT) and Edmund 'Ironside'.

shaken Canute, as he pursued the beaten but indomitable English King into western Mercia; it certainly shook Canute's English and Danish councillors, many of whom could never expect to enjoy total peace of mind as long as Edmund kept fighting. Though it was in the councillors' own interests to press for the total defeat of Edmund, they advised Canute that the wisest course to take was to negotiate with him for a peaceful partition of the English kingdom.

After an exchange of messengers, hostages and vows to confirm a truce, the two Kings met on an island in the River Severn at Alney, near Deerhurst in Gloucestershire, and the kingdom created by Edward the Elder and Athelstan was carved up between them. The lion's share went to Canute: Northumbria, Mercia, the Danelaw, East Anglia, and Essex with London. Edmund, for all his iron resolution, was decidedly not negotiating from a position of strength, as Alfred had been after the capture of London in 886. Edmund's confirmation as king in Wessex, however, was an enormous improvement on the submission of the entire country to Sweyn only three years before. Exactly as Alfred's treaty had done after

886, the Alney treaty of 1016 confirmed Wessex as the rallying-point for all free Englishmen not prepared to live under Danish rule.

In their meeting at Alney, Edmund and Canute exchanged personal gifts and courtesies, each formally recognizing the other's rights and status as king. Certainly Edmund needed the respite offered by the treaty; quite apart from the war-weariness of his people, it would take time to get the southern English accustomed to their new status, with its promise for the future balanced by the manifest dangers of the present. Above all the royal line of succession was, at this moment, most dangerously fragile. The athelings Alfred and Edward were too young to rule and were out of the kingdom anyway, in Normandy; Edmund's last surviving brother, Eadwig, had done nothing to establish himself as a fit candidate for the throne. Edmund's own dramatic marriage to Aldgyth in 1015 had already produced one son, Edmund, and by the autumn of 1016 Aldgyth was pregnant again (with another son who was born in 1017 and named Edward). Only the passage of time could repair the temporary vulnerability of the ancient ruling line of Saxon England.

After the abject and total collapse of the kingdom under his father, Edmund's restoration of national morale in 1015–16, and his securing of Wessex as an independent English realm, must be accounted one of the most magnificent achievements of any English king. What the sequel would have been is anybody's guess, but probably the aftermath of 1016 would have been a protracted duel between Edmund and Canute for the mastery of all England, similar to the personal crusade waged by Philip Augustus of France against the English Plantagenets 175 years later. However, all hopes for a continued English recovery were blotted out by Edmund's unexpected death on 30 November 1016. They buried him at Glastonbury, beside his grandfather Edgar the Peaceable. For the second time in three years, all England was left with no choice but to accept the alien rule of a Danish king.

8 Canute, Harold 'Harefoot' and Harthacanute 1016-1042

CANUTE OF DENMARK turned out to be one of the most welcome surprises the English have ever had. After Edmund Ironside died at the end of 1016, they accepted Canute as king because they had no choice; Canute already had two-thirds of the country in his power, and was backed by an enormous fleet and army whose potential destructive power made further resistance unthinkable. Within two years, however, both army and fleet had been paid off and sent back to Denmark, and Canute was reigning as a god-fearing English king, for all the world as though the blood of Edgar the Peaceable flowed in his veins. In fact this reformed Viking held up Edgar as his model, ordered the English to obey Edgar's laws and gave them a reign of national 'peace with honour' excelling not only that of Edgar but also that of any previous English king. From being a destroyer of the Christian world, Canute became one of its greatest ornaments. It was an extraordinary reformation and when he died in 1035 he was sincerely missed.

Born in 995, Canute was six years younger than his deadly rival of 1016, Edmund Ironside. He made his name during his father's wars in England, and his early prowess as a Viking warrior chief in the classic tradition, scourging the English land and people, was chanted by the *skalds* of the Scandinavian world:

Destroyer of the chariot of the sea, you were of no great age when you pushed off your ships. Never, younger than you, did prince set out to take his part in war. Chief, you made ready your armoured ships, and were daring beyond measure. In your rage, Cnut, you mustered the red shields at sea ...

You carried the shield of war, and so dealt mightily, chief. I do not think, O Prince, that you cared much to sit at ease. Lord of the Jutes, you smote the race of Edgar in that raid. King's son, you dealt them a cruel blow. You are given the name of stubborn ...

You made war in green Lindsey, Prince. The vikings wrought there what violence they would. In your rage, withstander of the Swedes, you brought sorrow upon the English, in *Helmingborg* to the west of the Ouse.

Young leader, you made the English fall close by the Tees. The deep dyke flowed over the bodies of Northumbrians. You broke the raven's sleep, waker of battle. Bold son of Sweyn, you led an attack at Sherstone, farther to the south.

There, I know, you took the Frisians' lives, breaker of the peace

PREVIOUS PAGES Canute rebuking his flattering courtiers by proving that he did not, in fact, have the power to halt the incoming tide. Over the centuries the point of this affectionate folk-tale has been lost, and the episode is usually cited today as a classic example of futile and ignorant arrogance.

of shields. You shattered Brentford with its habitations. Edmund's noble offspring met with deadly wounds. The Danish force shot down the men with spears, but you pursued the flying host.

Mighty Scylding, you fought a battle beneath the shield at *Assatun* [Ashingdon]. The blood-crane got morsels brown [with blood]. Prince, you won renown enough with your great sword, north of *Danaskogar*, but to your men it seemed a slaughter indeed. . . . Still you pressed on, blunting swords upon weapons; they could not defend their strongholds when you attacked. The bow screamed loud. You won no less renown, driver of the leaping steed of the roller, on Thames's bank. The wolf's jaw knew this well . . .

This was all good, stirring stuff, but any Englishman who heard this saga at its first recital probably experienced a sense of complacency rather than shame. For as early as 1018, Canute's second year as king of England, a rather different message was composed for the benefit of his subjects:

> This is the ordinance which the councillors determined and devised according to many good precedents; and that took place as soon as King Canute with the advice of his councillors completely established peace and friendship between the Danes and the English and put an end to all their former strife. In the first place, the councillors determined that above all things they would ever honour one God and steadfastly hold one Christian faith, and would love King Canute with due loyalty and zealously observe Edgar's laws. And they agreed that they would, with God's help, investigate further at leisure what was necessary for the nation, as best they could. Now we wish to make clear what can benefit us in religious and secular concerns, let him pay heed who will. Let us very resolutely turn from sins and eagerly atone for our misdeeds and duly love and honour one God and steadfastly hold one Christian faith and diligently avoid every heathen practice.

These two sources, so completely opposed in spirit, sum up the magnificent paradox that was Canute. He was a prodigy, a historic contradiction in terms, the greatest of the civilized Viking kings – and Saxon England was the most powerful ingredient in his civilizing. Although conditioned from boyhood to make use of applied violence in every useful form, treachery not excepted, Canute realized from the start that the iron fist could only be used to conquer England: it would not serve to rule the land. Nor, indeed, was force necessary once the English realized that their ruler was a trustworthy lord. Canute instinctively knew that the formula for governing Saxon England was a properly observed social contract between king and subjects. King Ethelred had violated that contract throughout his reign; Edmund Ironside, the toughest enemy Canute ever knew, had virtually repaired it by the time of his death; he, Canute, was determined to restore it in full. And he started by treating the Witan of England not as the mouthpiece of a conquered people, but as the trusted council of a realm of which he was supremely honoured to become king.

The chronicler Florence of Worcester describes the careful skill – the ultimate sanction of brute force was kept well out of sight – with which Canute engineered the legality of his accession to the kingdom:

And after [Edmund's] death, King Cnut gave orders that all the bishops and ealdormen and leading men, and all the nobles of the English people, were to be assembled at London. When they had come before him, he, as if in ignorance, questioned shrewdly those who had been witnesses between him and Edmund when they had made the pact of friendship and the division of the kingdom between them, how he and Edmund had spoken together concerning the latter's brothers and sons; whether his brothers and sons should be allowed to reign after their father in the kingdom of the West Saxons, if Edmund were to die in Cnut's lifetime. And they said that they knew beyond doubt that King Edmund had entrusted no portion of his kingdom to his brothers, either in his life or at his death; and they said that they knew that Edmund wished Cnut to be the supporter and protector of his sons, until they were old enough to reign. In truth, God is to witness, they gave false testimony, and lied deceitfully, imagining that he would be more gracious to them because of their lying, and that they would receive a big reward from him. Some of these false witnesses were put to death not long afterwards by that same king. Then after the above-mentioned enquiry, King Cnut tried to obtain from the aforesaid nobles oaths of fealty. And they swore to him that they would elect him as their king and humbly obey him, and make a payment to his army; and, accepting a pledge from his bare hand, along with oaths from the leading men of the Danes, they utterly renounced the brothers and sons of Edmund, and repudiated them as kings.

OPPOSITE Canterbury beseiged by the Danes in 1011, during the disastrous reign of Ethelred 'Evil-Counsel' – a stained glass window in Canterbury Cathedral.

160

This piece of stage-management not only gave Canute's accession the stamp of legality: it helped him sort out, in his own mind, which of the English leaders were turncoats and opportunists, and which were troubled patriots only accepting him as king for want of any alternative. He also knew that it was the last drop of England's humiliation as a nation – and he made it the last.

Canute's first 'administration' was a temporary one, dividing the kingdom into four. As king, he kept Wessex, heartland of the kingdom, for himself. Three great earldoms accounted for the rest of the realm: East Anglia went to Thorkel, Northumbria to Eric, and Mercia – for the moment – was handed back to Eadric Streona. Canute had no illusions about Eadric, but before dealing faithfully with England's foremost professional traitor he gave Eadric a little more rope. Eadric's first piece of advice to the new king was to have the last brother of Edmund Ironside, Eadwig, exiled and assassinated; he also advised Canute to kill Edmund's sons, Edward and Edgar, but to have this done abroad, 'because it would be a great disgrace to him for them to perish in England'. This told Canute all he needed to know about the Earl of Mercia, and for the rest of 1017 Eadric, all unknowing, was living on borrowed time.

Canute then balanced the liquidation of Eadwig with a much more positive gesture: in July 1017 he married Ethelred's widow, Emma of Normandy. As a dowager queen, Emma must have had some say in the matter, and presumably agreed to the marriage because it offered the best chance of safeguarding her sons by Ethelred, the athelings Edward and Alfred. She must also have found it hard to bear that her second marriage, like her first to Ethelred in 1002, was followed within months by treachery and murder on the part of her new husband, for in December 1017 Canute eliminated the individuals whom he had had marked down for months:

And at the Lord's Nativity, when he was in London, he gave orders for the perfidious ealdorman Eadric to be killed in the palace, because he feared to be at some time deceived by his treachery, as his former lords Ethelred and Edmund had frequently been deceived; and he ordered his body to be thrown over the wall of the city and left unburied. Along with him were killed, though guiltless, Ealdorman Northman, son of Ealdorman Leofwine and thus brother to Earl Leofric, Aethelweard, son of Ealdorman Aethelmaer, and Brihtric, son of the Devonshire magnate Aelfeah. The king appointed Leofric ealdorman in the place of his brother Northman, and afterwards held him in great esteem.

Thus Florence of Worcester, voicing the satisfaction of all Englishmen at the thoroughly merited demise of Eadric Streona. In the following year, Canute rounded out his accession settlement with his people, exacting a final crushing Danegeld of 72,000 pounds – with another 10,500 pounds from London – with which to pay off the Danish army and fleet. But this last agonizing turn of the screw was soothed by the King's promise that henceforth he intended to rule through the medium of Edgar's laws. Naturally, it took time before the English started to accept that Canute meant what he said, but the gesture was a reassuring one.

In the opening years of Canute's reign a major worry for the English Witan was Canute's natural concern with his extensive responsibilities outside England. He returned to Denmark in 1019–20 to make sure of that kingdom on his brother's death, and his subsequent efforts to make sure of his supremacy over the whole of Scandinavia caused the constant worry that the King would use England as a combined treasury, arsenal and recruiting centre for his Scandinavian wars. Though English volunteers did fight for Canute in Norway and Sweden, this worry also proved unfounded.

The most endearing documents of Canute's reign are the long letters he sent to the Witan whenever he left the kingdom. Their striking similarity of style to the edicts of Ethelred suggests that he appreciated the fluency of the English 'civil service', and took care to take a staff of English clerks with him on his travels in order to strike the right note when communicating with the Witan. These letters by the overlord of the Viking world suggest nothing so much as a considerate father, summoned abroad on business, letting his family know that he was all right, that everything was going well, that he was keeping in close touch with their interests, and that he would be back as soon as he could. This is how he opened his letter to the English on his first trip overseas, to Denmark in 1019–20:

King Cnut greets in friendship his archbishops and his diocesan

163

bishops, and Earl Thorkel and all his earls, and all his people, whether men of a twelve hundred wergild or a two hundred, ecclesiastic and lay, in England.

And I inform you that I will be a gracious lord and a faithful observer of God's rights and just secular law.

I have borne in mind the letters and messages which Archbishop Lifing brought me from Rome from the Pope, that I should everywhere exalt God's praise and suppress wrong and establish full security, by that power which it has pleased God to give me.

Since I did not spare my money as long as hostility was threatening you, I have now with God's help put an end to it with

my money.

Then I was informed that greater danger was approaching us than we liked at all; and then I went myself with the men who accompanied me to Denmark, from where the greatest injury had come to you, and with God's help I have taken measures so that never henceforth shall hostility reach you from there as long as you support me rightly and my life lasts.

Now I thank Almighty God for his help and his mercy, that I have so settled the great dangers which were approaching us that we need fear no danger to us from there; but [we may reckon] on full help and deliverance, if we need it.

John Martin's splendid painting of Canute demonstrating his inadequacies as a tidal expert.

lapoar rcðul· patn onpðnum pide lecgan· hponne
me gemitte man rcyldigne· pme flon oððe nicoh.
rædðe gamonige· bnodon cpealmat· ic hir blod agloat.
onlon onlondan· puto dæge pirrum· adlmat me
fnam ouguðe· jadpirat fnom· tande minum· me
to aldon banan· plondeð pnadna rum· ic apynged
rcðul· plooð of gerylðe· pinne hplonfan.

noe frume. ⁊pa hine nergend hehc. hynde þam hal
gan. hebron cyninge ongan. orort lice þ hor pyrcan
micle mihre cirte. magum ræzde. þpær þrulic þing
þrodum toþrund. nede pite. hie neþohron þær. ge
ræih þaymb pinqia þorn. þær ſært metod. gibron
hura mært. gcano hlipigtan. inagn ⁊utan. tondan
lime. gerærtnod pið flode. fæn noſt. þy relſtan.
þir ryndrig cynn. Symle bið þy hſandra. þelic hrþoh
þæſh. ⁊plaurce ſæ rcyrtumar. ſpið on bſiutud.

It was, of course, propaganda, but of a high order. On his return from Denmark Canute continued to make it clear that the bad old days were over, though he appreciated that not everything about them was a matter of shame to the English. In 1020, for example, he dedicated a lavish new church at Ashingdon, scene of the great battle in 1016 – a gesture which commemorated not only his own victory there, but the gallantry of the English themselves under their late king. And in 1023 he gladly supported a solemn ceremony of atonement for one of the blackest crimes committed by the Danes during the last years of their conquest of England: the murder of Archbishop Aelfheah, sanctified ten years after the event. Canute presided over the magnificent and solemn translation of the saint's remains from St Paul's in London to Canterbury. As the *Chronicle* has it:

> ... the illustrious King, and the Archbishop and diocesan bishops, and the earls, and very many ecclesiastics and also lay-folk, conveyed his holy body across the Thames to Southwark, and there entrusted the holy martyr to the archbishop and his companions. And they then bore him with a distinguished company and happy jubilation to Rochester. Then on the third day Queen Emma came with her royal child Hardacnut, and they then all conveyed the holy archbishop with much glory and joy and songs of praise into Canterbury, and thus brought him with due ceremony into Christ Church on 11 June.

The ceremonial translation of St Aelfheah in 1023 marked, in effect, Canute's official reconciliation with the English people. The last occasion of a similar ceremony had been the official funeral of St Edward at Shaftesbury, back in 979; but the ceremonial of 1023 was in total contrast to the guilt-ridden proceedings at the outset of Ethelred's reign. It is significant that this is the longest entry in the *Chronicle* for the reign of Canute, which is virtually a carbon copy of Edgar's reign as far as the sparseness of entries is concerned. Like the description of Edgar, nothing else testifies so eloquently to the tranquillity of England in the time of Canute. He had promised his people to give them peace and justice as Edgar had done, and he kept his word to the letter.

Canute fulfilled his traditional function as defender of the law

Sound though it was as currency, Canute's coinage can hardly be called beautiful. About the only recognizable feature on this penny is the sign of the Cross.

with his monumental overhaul of the laws of the land, the longest law code in the entire history of Saxon England to survive and, like those of Alfred and Offa of Mercia, an enduring encyclopedia of legal precedent. This law code also belongs to the early 1020s, and it is, suitably for the atmosphere of the time, a dual recognition of English and Danish procedure with deference to the Church and the laws of God over all.

The most prestigious event of Canute's reign was his journey to Rome in 1027 to attend the coronation of the new Emperor, Conrad. This visit completed the transmogrification of the Viking warrior chief into the most renowned ruler of northern Europe, conferring on equal terms with Pope and Emperor in the capital of Christendom. As far as England was concerned, the visit was without precedent; none of the Saxon kings had ever achieved such eminence.

Canute marked the occasion with another of his letters to the

Witan, one positively bursting with thoroughly deserved pride:

> Be it known to you, that there was a great assembly of nobles at the celebration of Easter, with the lord Pope John and the Emperor Conrad, namely all the princes of the nations from Mount Garganus [on the Adriatic] to the sea nearest [to us]; and they all received me with honour and honoured me with precious gifts; and especially was I honoured by the emperor with various gifts and costly presents, with vessels of gold and silver and silk robes and very costly garments.
>
> I therefore spoke with the emperor and the lord pope and the princes who were present, concerning the needs of all the peoples of my whole kingdom, whether English or Danes, that they might be granted more equitable law and greater security on their way to Rome, and that they should not be hindered by so many barriers on the way and so oppressed by unjust tolls; and the emperor and King Rodulf [of Burgundy], who chiefly had dominion over those barriers, consented to my demands; and all the princes confirmed by edicts that my men, whether merchants or others travelling for the sake of prayer, should go to and return from Rome in safety with firm peace and just law, free from hindrances by barriers and tolls. . . .
>
> Indeed, all the things which I demanded for the benefit of my people from the lord pope and from the emperor and from King Rodulf and the other princes through whose lands our way to Rome lies, they most willingly granted, and also confirmed what they had granted with an oath, with the witness of four archbishops and twenty bishops and an innumerable multitude of dukes and nobles who were present.
>
> Therefore I give most hearty thanks to Almighty God, that I have successfully accomplished all that I had desired, just as I had designed, and have carried out my vows to my satisfaction.

After advising the Witan that he would be returning to England only after a preliminary visit to Denmark in order to leave that kingdom in good – and hence safe – order, Canute proceeded:

> But I send ahead this letter, in order that all the people of my kingdom may be gladdened at my success, because, as you yourselves know, I have never spared – nor will I spare in the future – to devote myself and my toil for the need and benefit of all my people.

As Canute's reign proceeded in peaceful state towards its close, warmed by the afterglow of the Rome 'summit', only one problem was left unresolved to trouble his subjects on his death: the succession. His own statecraft had sufficed for him to rule, more as a president than as a king or emperor, over an uneasy and decidedly temporary enforced union between England, Denmark, Norway and Sweden. It was a foregone conclusion that his Scandinavian kingdoms would go their own ways when he died, but this would not leave England immune from claimants from across the North Sea. Canute's private life had complicated the succession further. By an English mistress taken during the conquest of England, Aelfgifu of Northampton, Canute had a son, Harold, with the cryptic but unpromising nickname of 'Harefoot'. His legitimate heir by Emma of Normandy was the prince Hardacnut, or Harthacanute as he is commonly anglicized. For once, a clear-cut will by the father of these two claimants to the English throne would have gone a long way towards making the succession smoother – but Canute had not defined his wishes when he died at Shaftesbury on 12 November 1035.

Harthacanute's first action showed that he would not be following his father's policy of 'England first': he crossed the North Sea to make certain of Denmark, leaving his mother and her supporters in the English Witan to defend his interests in England. The most prominent of these was the ambitious magnate whom Canute, in his last years, had created earl of Wessex: Earl Godwine. He headed the party in the Witan which declared for Harthacanute in the crucial session of the council held at Oxford after Canute's death. But they were out-voted by Earl Leofric of Mercia, who opposed Harold's succession as king but was willing to consider him as a regent, with Queen Emma maintaining a royal household and force of 'house-carls' or armed retainers in Harthacanute's name at Winchester.

The latter proposal carried the day, despite the efforts of Godwine to block it. Such an unprecedented experiment was asking for trouble, which was not long in coming. Harold sent an armed force to Winchester to seize the treasure of Canute, and had himself proclaimed 'full king over all England'. His short five-year reign, in comparison to the peace Canute had

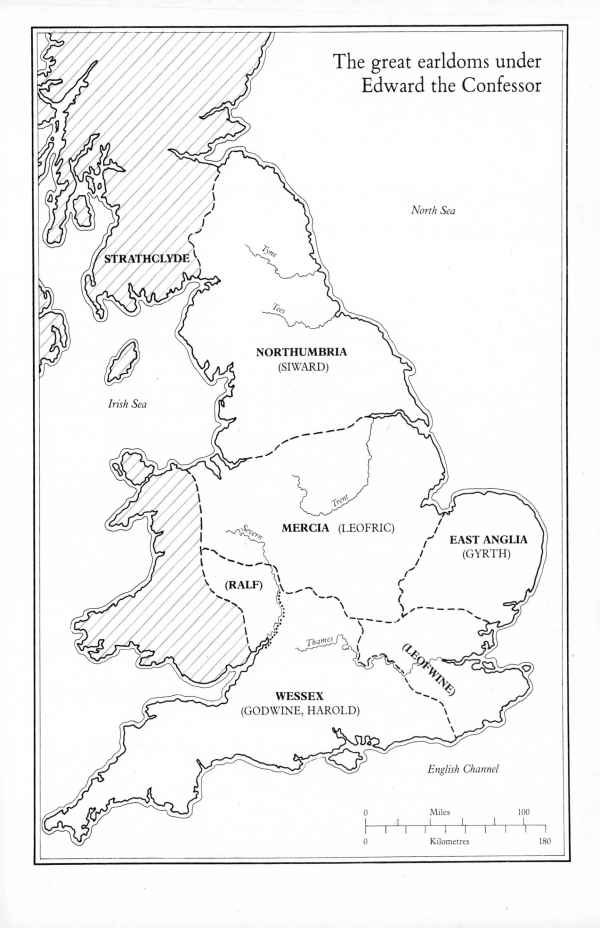

The great earldoms under
Edward the Confessor

North Sea

STRATHCLYDE

Tyne

Tees

Irish Sea

NORTHUMBRIA
(SIWARD)

Trent

MERCIA (LEOFRIC)

EAST ANGLIA
(GYRTH)

Severn

(RALF)

Thames

(LEOFWINE)

WESSEX
(GODWINE, HAROLD)

English Channel

| 0 | | Miles | | 100 |
| 0 | | Kilometres | | 180 |

maintained in England, stands out as a time of lengthening shadows: wars with the Welsh in which Earl Leofric's brother was killed, and a natural disaster – a terrible gale. The most momentous event, whose aftermath rumbled on for many years, took place in 1036 and reminded the English that the sons of Canute were not the only claimants to the throne. The atheling Alfred, one of the sons of Ethelred by Emma, made the fatal mistake of coming to England 'wishing', the *Chronicle* says, 'to go to his mother who was in Winchester'. On his arrival in England, Alfred was arrested and his companions scattered – the lucky ones. Those taken with Alfred were either sold as slaves, tortured to death, mutilated, blinded, or scalped. Alfred's end was no less hideous: his eyes were put out as he was being taken by ship to imprisonment in Ely, and he died of the shock. It was said that these atrocities were committed by Earl Godwine, the former supporter of Harthacanute, in order to ingratiate himself

174

with Harold. This left the atheling Edward as the only surviving son of Ethelred, and support for him grew as the sons of Canute continued to dispel all the goodwill built up by their mighty father.

By the end of 1037, Harold's position was apparently secure. He had viciously disposed of his most dangerous potential rival to appear in England, and in 1037 the last supporters of Harthacanute's claim to the English throne renounced their allegiance and pledged support for Harold. He emphasized his supremacy in the same year by expelling Queen Emma from England. She settled at Bruges where Harthacanute, having finally obtained a settlement with the new king of Norway, Magnus, joined her in 1039 as a preliminary to building up an army of invasion. But the English were spared the inevitable consequence of such a venture – civil war – by Harold's death at Oxford on 17 March 1040.

Harthacanute was King of England for barely twenty-four months, and for the English his reign was remembered as twenty-four months too long. Harold had been bad enough, but Harthacanute behaved precisely as it had been feared Canute would when he succeeded Edmund; he treated England as the king of Denmark's financial milch-cow. When he had dispersed the great Danish fleet after the wars of conquest, Canute had maintained a modest fleet of forty warships for the defence of England, for which the English were required to pay with a ship-tax assessed at eight marks to the rowlock. Canute had subsequently reduced the size of the fleet to sixteen ships, and Harold had kept it at that level. On his accession Harthacanute, however, obsessed with Denmark and its far higher naval requirements, promptly increased the fleet to sixty-two ships – a near-quadrupling of taxation which pushed wheat prices through the roof and provoked a howl of anguish from the *Chronicle*: 'All who had wanted him before were then ill-disposed towards him.'

The picture of Harthacanute which has come down to us is that of a heavy-handed, uncaring ruler with his mind elsewhere. 'And he did nothing worthy of a king as long as he ruled,' is the *Chronicle's* savage epitaph – a dismissal which not even the hapless Ethelred had ever had levelled against him in writing. Also remembered for having his predecessor's body exhumed and flung into a swamp, Harthacanute ravaged the whole of Worcestershire in 1041 in revenge for two of his house-carls, killed while trying to collect the King's hated ship-tax. The infuriated citizens had chased the house-carls into the city minster and lynched them there, heedless of the sanctuary law or the King's savage reprisal. There is a very good chance that if Harthacanute's reign had lasted much longer his ship-tax – like that of Charles I, 600 years later – would have provoked civil war and the deposition of the King. By far the most effective act of Harthacanute's brief reign was his summoning to England of half-brother, the atheling Edward. to share in the ruling of the kingdom. This would, of course, facilitate Harthacanute's instant departure for Denmark should events there have required it, but it also effectively solved the succession problem for the first time in over half a century. Harthacanute was unmarried and childless.

The end came in June 1042 and was vividly described by Florence of Worcester:

Hardacnut, king of the English, was standing at the wedding-feast given at the place called Lambeth by Osgod Clapa, a great lord, on the occasion of the joyful marriage of his daughter, Gytha, to Tofig, surnamed Pruda, a Danish magnate. Full of health and mirth, he was drinking with the bride and guests when suddenly, even in the act of drinking, he fell down, and remained speechless until 8 June when he died. He was carried to Winchester and there buried by the side of King Cnut, his father.

'And before he was buried', adds the *Chronicle*, 'all the people chose Edward as king in London. May he hold it as long as God will grant it him.'

9 Edward 'the Confessor'

and Harold Godwinesson 1042-1066

O F THE INNUMERABLE KINGS of England who have had their memories traduced over the passing of the centuries, Edward 'The Confessor' is high on the list. His very nickname preserves the image of an unworldly greybeard, obsessed with religious devotion in an age which demanded kings of sterner stuff. Charles Kingsley's novel *Hereward the Wake* is a typical offender, with its virile young hero sneering at the 'pious driveller' and 'bellwether' disgracing the throne of England. In fact Kingsley's fictional Hereward and the real King Edward had one glaringly obvious trait in common: in a violent and treacherous century, both of them were past masters in the art of survival. By the time he returned to England in 1040, Edward had already avoided death in battle, betrayal or political assassination during twenty-five years in exile. When he became king two years later he faced difficulties such as none of the Saxon kings before him had known: a tortuous combination of trouble from over-mighty subjects inside the kingdom and threats from over-mighty neighbours outside. It was thoroughly fitting that Edward lived to a revered old age; he had survived everything, and the odds against him doing so had always stood forbiddingly high.

There was a tough resilience about Edward which had been quite lacking in his father Ethelred and this clearly came from his mother, Emma of Normandy – that formidable lady who married two kings of England, bore two more and remained a political force until her death in 1052, half a century after she had come to England as Ethelred's bride. It is no surprise to find mother and son at loggerheads throughout the first ten years of Edward's reign, though the reasons were as much political as the natural collision of two determined characters. Edward was born within two years at most after the marriage of Ethelred and Emma, and as recounted in the previous chapter his boyhood was passed in a decade which saw his father's misrule bring the English kingdom to total defeat at the hands of the Danes. Edward would have been about ten years old when his mother took him, with his younger brother Alfred, to safety in her native Normandy. Within weeks King Ethelred, rejected by his despairing people, had joined his family in exile.

To have a father of whom one is ashamed must be one of the most corrosive experiences any child can suffer, and it must

PREVIOUS PAGES From the 'Life of St Edward': the king's return to England (LEFT) and his coronation.

have been very difficult indeed for a growing prince to have felt proud of a father like Ethelred. Among all the questions we would like answered about Edward's boyhood, one of the most interesting is to whom, apart from his mother, he looked for inspiration. There seems to have been little or no contact between Edward and Alfred and their half-brothers by Ethelred's first marriage. Indeed, the will of Ethelred's eldest son, the atheling Athelstan, pointedly omits any bequest to Edward, Alfred or Emma, while remembering his full brothers Edmund and Eadwig, his foster-mother Aelfswith, and 'the soul of Aelfthryth my grandmother, who brought me up'. If there was active estrangement between the sons of Ethelred, this cannot have been ameliorated by the exclusion of the elder athelings from Ethelred's surprise restoration in the spring of 1014. For it was during the negotiations for Ethelred's return to England that the young Edward was given his first chance of serving his future subjects.

When the messengers of the Witan arrived in Normandy with the news of recall, Ethelred, regrettably true to form, declined to act with boldness and return immediately to England himself. He sent Edward back with the messengers instead, doubtless calculating that the boy's arrival would disarm opposition both in the Witan and among the people. In view of Ethelred's pathological fear of treachery it was a shocking risk for him to take with his son and heir, even though everything passed off well. Certainly Edward carried out his mission perfectly, and his demeanour may well have prompted the spontaneous decision by the Witan to outlaw every Danish king from England for ever.

Within two years of this debut, however, Edward and Alfred were back in Normandy and their prospects looked gloomier than ever. Their father was dead and their half-brother Edmund was fighting desperately to save England from Canute of Denmark. By the end of 1016 Edmund was dead as well and Canute was stage-managing the Witan into electing him king of England. Edward and Alfred now represented only one of three possible claims to the English throne. Apart from themselves there was their last surviving half-brother in England, the atheling Eadwig, and the baby son of Edmund Ironside, the atheling Edmund (soon to be joined by yet another

181

atheling: Edward). This field was reduced to four when Canute had Eadwig killed at the end of 1017, but this did not simplify matters for Edward and Alfred. Their mother had by now married the arch-enemy, Canute, and soon presented him with a direct heir, Harthacanute. As far as their prospects of ever returning to their birthright in England were concerned, Edward and Alfred seemed fated to live out their lives in dynastic limbo, as exiles. The most that could be said for their mother's second marriage was that it would probably spare them from a visit by Canute's assassins.

They grew to manhood in Normandy under the effective guardianship of their uncle, Duke Richard II (996–1026). While protecting the persons of his nephews, Richard had no intention of sponsoring their political claims in England by flouting his second brother-in-law, the mighty Canute, of whom he remained an ally. By the time Canute died in 1035, however, the prospects for Edward and Alfred had changed considerably. The alignment between Normandy and Canute had lapsed after Richard's death, and the athelings in Normandy had attracted enough companions for them to consider an armed descent on England. It is possible that such an attempt lay behind the arrest and murder of Alfred in England in 1036. Two Norman accounts claim that Edward had actually tried an earlier landing at Southampton with forty ships, only to withdraw when he realized that his strength was insufficient. (If true, this makes Edward not merely the only Saxon king to have been reared abroad, but the only one to have assaulted England with a fleet of longships, like any Viking.) The same Norman sources affirm that Alfred then landed in Kent with a stronger force, only to be betrayed by Earl Godwine and savagely put to death, a grim example to deter Edward from trying again.

An obsequious biographer of Queen Emma gives the story another twist, claiming that the evil Harold 'Harefoot' lured Alfred over to England by forging a letter from Emma to her sons, urging one of them: 'Come to me speedily and privately, to receive from me wholesome counsel'. If the forgery story is true, the shock of Alfred's murder must have affected Edward with particularly violent emotions: not just grief over his brother's death and shame at having been deceived, but guilt at

ABOVE Hunting scene, with wild boar as the quarry. According to one source Edward, an enthusiastic horseman and devotee of the chase, 'was really delighted by the baying and scrambling of the hounds'.

RIGHT The Confessor's better-known image, as the saintly founder of Westminster Abbey.

having helped bring about Alfred's death by not insisting on going himself. Edward could hardly have forgotten that he had been placed in similar jeopardy by his own father twenty-two years before. A guilty sense of being in divine favour while his brother lay buried in Ely with his eyes ripped out might well have accentuated Edward's natural piety.

Certainly the cards were dealt shrewdly to Edward after the death of Alfred. The misdeeds of Harold and Harthacanute steadily undermined loyalty in England towards Canute's heirs, generating a ground swell of nostalgic loyalty towards the ancient English ruling line of which Edward was now far and away the most prominent heir. His summons to return to England as Harthacanute's co-ruler not only boosted this loyalty but gave him a much-needed 'familiarization course' in the country to which he had been a stranger for so long. And it paved the way to Edward's unanimous election as Harthacanute's successor in June 1042.

By the time he ascended his father's throne, Edward knew very well that there could be no question of turning the clock

185

Edward's royal seal, capturing the uneasy balance between the sword and the dove of peace in which he contrived to keep his kingdom. That Edward preferred the pompous Greek title *basileus* to the more modest *rex* (king) hints that the Confessor was far more concerned with his royal dignity than is popularly believed.

back to Ethelred's time. The England of his grandfather Edgar's reign had gone for good, and in its stead was the Anglo-Danish realm of Canute: the England of the great earls, Siward of Northumbria, Leofric of Mercia, and Godwine of Wessex. The very fact that the ancient core of the realm, Wessex, had been reduced in status from a kingdom to an earldom, was sufficient indication of how much England had changed under Canute. Every king of England from Edward the Elder to Edmund Ironside had known that the allegiance of Wessex was the cornerstone of his power; but Edward the Confessor had no such foundation. Wessex in his reign was the jealously guarded preserve of Earl Godwine, who used his earldom as a scaffolding from which to bend the king's policies in his own favour.

In 1040 Godwine had given a convincing demonstration of his cunning and power. The new king, Harthacanute, had threatened to punish Godwine for his part in the murder of Alfred, the King's half-brother, but Godwine slid out of trouble

186

with ease. Knowing Harthacanute's obsession with the fleet, Godwine presented the King with a spanking new warship complete with gilded prow, luxury tackle, a full stock of weapons and eighty picked soldiers whose persons and magnificent weapons glittered with gold. He also swore before the Witan that he had never wished for or advised Alfred's mutilation and death: this had been all Harold Harefoot's idea, and he had merely been following Harold's orders. Godwine emerged from the incident with his lands and power intact; but Edward now knew for certain that Godwine had been the instrument of Alfred's death, even if this had been done by royal command, and Edward was not a man who could be bought off with splendid gifts and cheap oaths. Edward was not only impervious to material bribery, he also took oaths very seriously indeed, which, considering how many of them he had seen broken during his life, is another tribute to his underlying strength of character.

In his first year as king, however, Edward needed the support of his leading earls, Godwine included. The problem was Denmark, now threatened with annexation by Magnus of Norway. In 1043 Edward was astounded to discover that his mother Emma, so far from rejoicing in her son's accession in England, had been intriguing to bring about the invasion of England by Magnus. The personal shock of having to accept the total revulsion which his mother clearly felt for her former life as Ethelred's queen – and the treasonable extent to which she was prepared to go in betraying her only surviving son by Ethelred – must have been hard for Edward to bear. Nevertheless he knew at once what had to be done, and acted decisively. He was backed by the irresistible trio of Siward, Leofric and Godwine, who in mid-November 1043 rode at Edward's side to Winchester and approved while Edward confiscated the immense treasure with which Emma had been invested by Harthacanute.

Edward's first act as king, this public despoiling and humiliation of his mother, earned him the warm approval of Canute's earls as well as the English people in general, who had no desire to have another Scandinavian king in England. The confiscation of Queen Emma's treasure was a shrewd and ostentatious blow aimed at England's biggest 'enemy within' at the outset of Edward's reign. It invites comparison with Ethelred's treacherous folly of the St Brice's Day massacre back in 1002. That ill-judged, wasteful butchery never earned Ethelred the praise and respect reaped by Edward after his timely action against Emma in November 1043. Edward treated her fairly afterwards, allowing her to live out the last ten years of her life in the comparatively modest state befitting the King's mother.

Clipping Emma's wings, however, did not remove the danger to England posed by Magnus of Norway, who remained an annual threat until his death in October 1047. Here again, Edward's behaviour was a heartening contrast to his father's, as every year he took personal command of the English fleet at its base at Sandwich, showing himself the true leader of his people as Ethelred had never done. Edward refused to commit his forces to the risky expedition to Denmark repeatedly advised by Godwine, accepting instead the advice of Leofric and Siward to stand on the defensive and husband the country's resources. Six years after his accession, Edward could proudly claim to have carried his country safely through the biggest crisis it had faced since 1016 – but he had been made to pay for it by appeasing Godwine's ambitions at home in order to ensure domestic security. A western earldom had been carved out of Wessex in 1043 for Godwine's eldest son, Sweyn, and in January 1045 Edward had taken Godwine's daughter Edith in marriage. Now beyond question the most powerful magnate in England after the King himself, Godwine addressed himself to his main ambition of making his family supreme throughout England, by flouting the King's authority at every turn and obtaining earldoms for the rest of his sons: Harold, Tostig, Gyrth, and Leofwine.

Faced with Godwine's transparent ambition, Edward's position was extraordinarily difficult. His marriage to Godwine's daughter was the smallest part of the problem; Edward, rising forty when he ascended the throne, was many years Edith's senior, and Edith never tried to play at politics as Emma of Normandy had done. The real problem was the fact that the Godwinessons were not moronic thugs, mutely obeying their father's bidding; they were talented soldiers and, with the exception of Sweyn, rakehell of the family, good administrators.

OPPOSITE Edward accepts Earl Godwine's daughter Edith as his queen. This political marriage did nothing to curb Edward's determination to oppose Godwine's naked ambition.
OVERLEAF The opening scene of the Bayeux Tapestry shows Edward bidding a formal farewell to Earl Harold ('Duke of the English') before the latter's departure for William's court in Normandy.

188

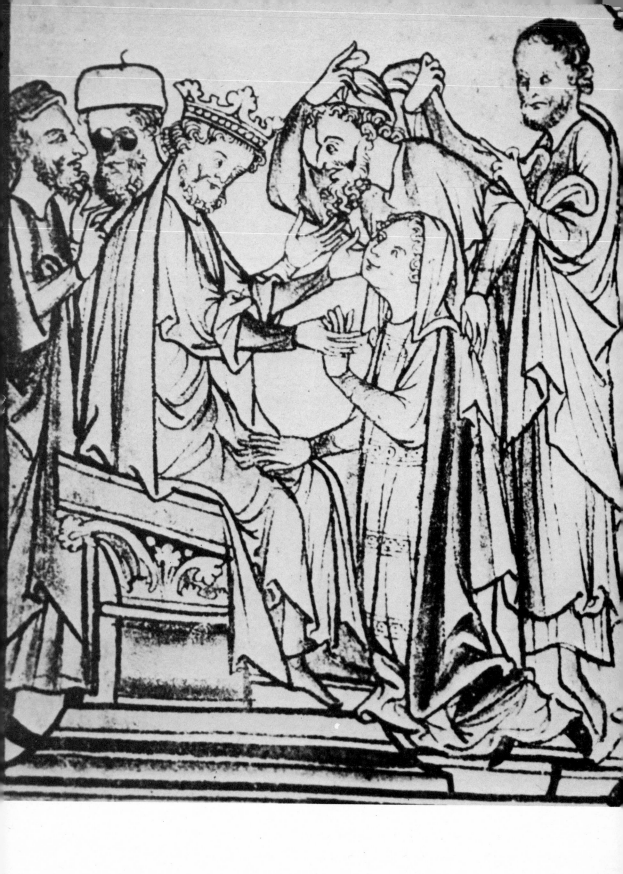

REX· VBI:HAROLD DVX·AN

An essential part of Edward's royal duties was to be seen as a fair and open-handed rewarder of talent, and he could not afford to ignore that of the Godwinessons.

By the end of 1050 Godwine's star was at its zenith. Sweyn was back in the country after having received his second pardon and recall (he had been exiled in 1046 for seducing an abbess, and again in 1049 for murdering his cousin Beorn). He now enjoyed a large earldom embracing all the former south-west shire of Mercia. Harold Godwinesson was also an earl – of East Anglia, Essex, Cambridgeshire and Huntingdonshire. However, these honours did not give the Godwine family unchallenged control of a monolithic power-block: they were riddled with smaller estates and earldoms granted by Edward to French courtiers in his favour (not all of them Normans, as is sometimes wrongly asserted of Edward). Godwine placed himself at the head of the widespread Anglo-Danish opposition to Edward's policy of appointing Frenchmen when a Frenchman was the best man for the job; but he could not stop Edward from appointing Robert, Abbot of Jumièges, as Archbishop of Canterbury in 1050. Nor could he prevent Edward from adding enormously to the royal prestige by making that perennial gesture to the taxpayer – defence cuts. Edward paid off nine of the fleet's fourteen ships in 1050, and in the following year he abolished the onerous tax, levied every year for the past thirty-nine years, which had paid for the standing military establishment of the Anglo-Danish kings.

In 1051 the latest attempt by Edward to assert his royal authority prompted Godwine to defy the King openly. During a state visit by Edward's brother-in-law, Count Eustace of Boulogne, a brawl occurred at Dover between the townsfolk and Eustace's retainers in which seven of the latter were killed. In atonement to his guest, Edward ordered Godwine to ravage Dover and its environs – the traditional royal punishment for riots capable of causing offence to foreigners. Godwine not only refused, but raised an army and defied Edward with it. Though initially taken by surprise, Edward called in Leofric and Siward, who negotiated a truce between the King and the Earl and called a session of the Witan at London to judge the whole matter fairly. As the supporters of Godwine began to waver, Edward called out the fyrd of all England, prompting desertions *en masse* from Godwine and his sons. When Godwine and Harold refused to appear before the Witan without a guarantee, secured by hostages, that they would be granted the king's peace, Edward merely gave them five days in which to leave England. Godwine and his wife Gytha, with Sweyn, Tostig and Gyrth, crossed the Channel to seek asylum at the court of Tostig's brother-in-law, Count Baldwin of Flanders. Edward then completed the official chastisement of the Godwine family by sending Queen Edith to the nunnery at Wherwell in Wessex.

In his tenth year as king, Edward had apparently gained a complete triumph over his enemy, but the abrupt removal of the Godwine family left an aching power vacuum in the south which the King now found virtually impossible to fill without weakening his own position. The exile of the Godwines was apparently followed by a spate of French appointments which caused widespread resentment and included the preferment of 'William the King's priest' (a Frenchman) as bishop of London. Another alarming straw in the wind, as Englishmen saw it, was the state visit to England in 1051 by the King's cousin, the eighteen-year-old Duke William of Normandy. This most unusual occasion (recorded by only one of the three contemporary texts of the *Chronicle*) could well have been more than a courtesy visit, a chance for Edward to show his gratitude to Normandy for having sheltered him as an exile. It could have been the moment when Edward offered William the succession to the English kingdom.

Edward and Edith were childless, and seemed likely to remain so; the only other surviving atheling was the second son of Edmund Ironside, Edward 'the Outlaw', as he was commonly known. This atheling, with his brother Edmund, had been reared in the remote court of Hungary to save him from assassination by Canute, and may as well have been living on Mars for all that anyone knew of his suitability as a candidate for the English throne. However, the king knew a great deal about Normandy and its young ruler, and had himself proved that a Norman prince (as Edward had virtually been when he returned to England) could provide a trouble-free succession. And it was essential for Edward to provide for this, because the Scandinavian world was now dominated by the last great warrior-hero of the Viking age: Harold Hardraada of Norway,

HIC RESIDET HAROLD REX ANGLORVM STIGANT ARCHI EPS

ABOVE The Bayeux
Tapestry shows the
coronation of Harold,
with Stigand at his side.
OPPOSITE Memorial
window to St Edward, in
Hereford Cathedral.

who would certainly not ignore the tempting prospect of an England under insecure leadership.

In 1052, however, Edward paid the penalty for having dispersed the armed forces maintained by his predecessors. The Godwines struck back with a surprise invasion of England in force, trapping Edward's tiny fleet in the Thames at London. Taken completely by surprise, Edward – like Godwine a year earlier – had no choice but to negotiate. He had to swallow the humiliation of reinstating Godwine and his sons in full (with the exception of Sweyn, who had died, most incongruously, while returning from a pilgrimage to Jerusalem) and taking back Queen Edith. The King was also obliged to dismiss his French appointees 'because', as the *Chronicle* sturdily affirms, 'they were most responsible for the disagreement between Earl Godwine and the King'.

Godwine himself only lived for seven months after his triumphant return; he collapsed while dining with the King on 15 April 1053. His death became the matter of legend: it was said that Edward had again accused the Earl of having murdered Alfred, and that Godwine angrily defended himself by inviting God to choke him with his next mouthful of bread if he were guilty. But although he had the satisfaction of outliving Godwine, Edward never fully recovered from the shock of the Earl's return and the overthrow of his policies. He was forced to acquiesce to what was, in effect, the fulfilment of Godwine's own policy: the establishment of the Godwinessons as the leading power in the land after the King, their brother-in-law, with Harold foremost among them.

The last ten years of Edward's reign saw Harold God-winesson established himself as the foremost general in the kingdom by virtue of his repeated victories over the Welsh king, Gruffyd. Although Edward was remembered for withdrawing more and more into religious concerns in these last years – his major obsession being the building of the magnificent new West Minster on the north bank of the Thames – he did all he possibly could to provide for the succession. Edward 'the Outlaw' was recalled to England in 1057; he died soon after his arrival, before he had even reached Edward's court, but left a son, Edgar, as an alternative candidate in the succession. And finally – perhaps in 1064 – Edward sent

OPPOSITE The Confessor's shrine in Westminster Abbey. The first two ceremonies held in the new 'West Minster' were the funeral of Edward and the coronation of Harold.

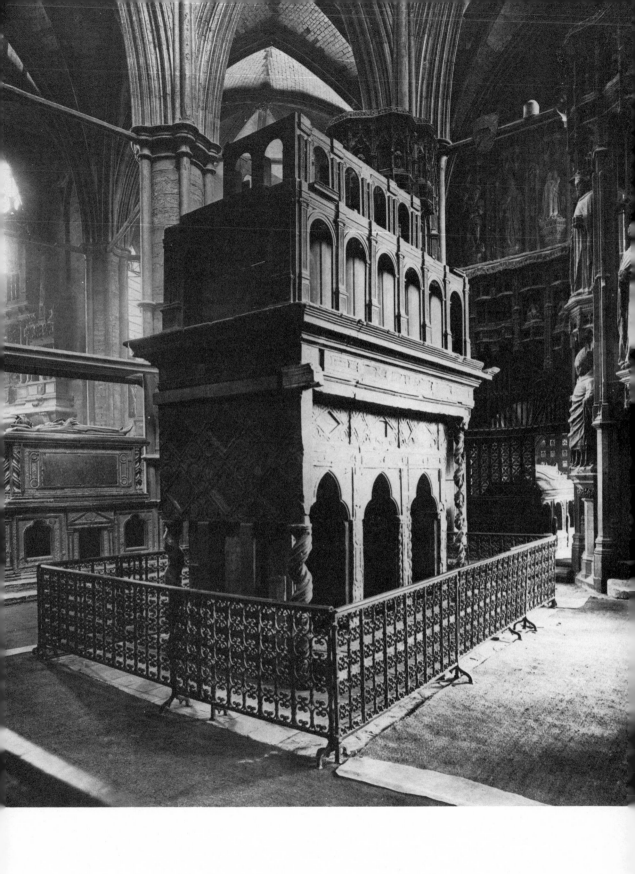

ODO·EPS·BACVLV·TENENS·:CONFOR· :HICEST·: VVLET

Confusion in the Norman ranks at Hastings. At right, William pushes back his helmet to show his men that he is still alive; at left Odo, the fighting Bishop of Bayeux, brandishes his mace at a retreating knight.

Harold across the Channel to the court of Duke William. The famous version of events preserved by the Bayeux Tapestry tells how Harold fought for William in Brittany and accepted arms from the Duke, which involved a nominal oath of allegiance, *before* publicly swearing his famous oath to support William's claim.

When Edward died on 5 January 1066 he had done all he could to arrange for the succession in the way he wanted. For a prince who began to reign when almost forty having spent nearly all his life in exile, Edward had put up an amazing performance in excessively difficult circumstances. Against the ruthless intriguers who were his contemporaries, his uprightness and piety made him stand out like a diamond in a dungheap, and he is remembered as the first patron saint of England. (Whether or not Edward would have been attributed saintly characteristics if he had been short, fat and bald, instead of tall and stately with a long white beard, is perhaps not an impertinent or irrelevant passing thought.) In his reign, Edward

198

had been helped by the last palpable burst of popular loyalty towards the Old English ruling house, but had learned that this was no longer absolute. His humiliation by Godwine in 1052 had come about largely because the English were not prepared to support the King in a cold-blooded civil war; they were becoming motivated, in times of crisis, by a growing acceptance of hard reality. It was this acceptance of reality that Harold exploited by immediately declaring himself as a candidate for the throne, and the verse eulogy of Edward in the *Chronicle* is deliberately misleading in its wording:

> ... And angels led
> His righteous soul to heaven's radiance.
> Yet the wise ruler entrusted the realm
> To a man of high rank, to Harold himself
> A noble earl who all the time
> Had loyally followed his lord's commands
> With words and deeds and neglected nothing
> That met the needs of the people's king.

Core of the English defence at Hastings: the 'shield-wall' formed by Harold's crack house-carls, their shields bristling with Norman arrows.

In January 1066 Harold Godwinesson might well have anticipated the famous words of William Pitt 700 years later: 'I know that I can save this country and that no one else can.' Only blind stupidity or supreme confidence could have induced anyone to embark on the task, and though Harold was certainly not renowned for stupidity, his problems were far greater than those which Edward had faced on his accession. Harold was confronted not by one invasion, but by two: Duke William from Normandy and Harold Hardraada from Norway. Instead of the solid backing which Edward had enjoyed from the earls Siward and Leofric, Harold had to overcome the hostility of the house of Leofric (now headed by Leofric's grandsons Edwin and Morcar) towards the house of Godwine. That hostility had been reflected in late 1065 by the expulsion of Tostig Godwinesson from his earldom of Northumbria and his replacement by Morcar. Harold could only wait and see whether Tostig, in his efforts to regain his lost earldom, would try to play a lone game or align himself with either William or Harold Hardraada.

From the very outset of his reign, Harold demonstrated that he was sensitive to the hostility which his father's ambitions had caused. Contemporaries stressed the almost indecent haste with which Harold's coronation followed Edward's funeral, but the new king took care not to be crowned by the notorious Archbishop Stigand of Canterbury, one of the greatest English embarrassments in 1066. Stigand was an intensely political animal, well known for having profitably hitched his wagon to Godwine's star. His position as Archbishop was unlawful in the eyes of the Church because he had assumed it while the previous incumbent, the exiled but properly-ordained Robert of Jumièges, was still alive. Harold therefore had himself crowned not by Stigand but by Ealdred, Archbishop of York, a fact which Norman propagandists found convenient to ignore. In the Bayeux Tapestry Harold is shown enthroned with Stigand at his side – a blatant perversion of the facts.

An even more positive gesture was Harold's repudiation of his mistress, Edith Swannehals ('Swan-neck'), by whom he had several children. He now married Edith, sister of Edwin and Morcar. This was reminiscent of his own sister's marriage to King Edward twenty years earlier, but was far more successful politically. Without the loyalty of Edwin and Morcar, Harold would have lost the north to Harold Hardraada when the latter invaded Northumbria later in the year. In addition to these sound political moves, Harold proved himself to be an energetic ruler by reforming the English coinage – always a sign of prudent concern for the country's economic future. There is little other concrete evidence of what sort of a king Harold would have made, however; all his preoccupations in 1066 centred on the defence of the realm.

The campaigns of 1066 are too well known for another detailed recital here. Despite his eventual defeat, they entitle Harold to be remembered among the greatest of England's medieval warrior-kings. His performance in racing north to break Harold Hardraada's invasion of Northumbria, then heading south to come within an inch of beating the Norman expeditionary force at Hastings, was prodigious. A few points, however, deserve comment. After waiting through the entire summer for his enemies to show their respective hands, Harold had seen his mobilization of the kingdom largely break down by the time Harold Hardraada and Tostig struck at York in early September. As the *Chronicle* admitted, 'the provisions of the people were gone, and nobody could stay there [in the south] any longer. Then they were allowed to go home.'

The defeat and death of Harold Hardraada and Tostig at Stamford Bridge on 25 September 1066, earned Harold of England a secure niche in Norse as well as English legend. Although the Bayeux Tapestry certainly does not suggest that Harold was 'a little man standing proudly in his stirrups', he won immortality for his defiance of Hardraada: '. . . only six feet of English soil; or, as he is a tall man, seven'. But it was largely thanks to the mauling which Edwin and Morcar had given the Norwegians at Fulford, only five days before Stamford Bridge, that Harold won his victory.

Of the ensuing Hastings campaign against William and the Normans, much has been made of Harold's burning haste to get to grips with the enemy instead of prudently waiting to gather all the forces he could have had. I believe that Harold was following the thoroughly prudent doctrine that enemy bridge-heads must be attacked before they grow too strong, or before the enemy has time to break out of them. Harold had fought

Apres seynt Edward le reg
na Harald le fiz Gode
wyn. Count de kent. a for
ea tort. ix. moys. dunk de
ent will bastard. e ly tol
yst la vye e le regne e quist
la tere. Harald gist al walthm.

Pur regna will bal
herd xxi. an. puis mo
rust e gist a kame en
mundye

with William's army in Brittany. He knew the mobility of the Norman knights, and what this could achieve. What is more, he had imitated it by putting his own crack corps of house-carls on horseback, thus gaining a mobility which William himself must have envied. The biggest myth about Hastings is that it was a foredoomed English defeat because of the excellence of the Norman military machine and the invincibility of the mounted knight against foot soldiers. This is sheer rubbish. Hastings was no more an inevitable Norman victory than Waterloo was an inevitable British victory; William had to stretch his powers of leadership to the utmost in order to prevent his army from dissolving in panic.

The cardinal error Harold made at Hastings was fighting on foot, Danish fashion, and getting himself killed. This was an act of bone-headed folly. It may well be that retreat from that hilltop 'by the hoary apple tree' had become impossible by the late afternoon of 14 October, but Harold should never have left himself without the option of escape. By dying with his men, Harold held true to the Scandinavian code of military honour, but his honour as an English king would have been even greater if he had fled from the field of Hastings to rally more forces and lead them against the invader again and again, as Alfred and Edmund Ironside had done. By flouting Edward's wishes and accepting the crown for himself, Harold had accepted responsibility for the people of England. His death at Hastings was the ultimate betrayal of that responsibility.

OPPOSITE Norman propaganda at its most outrageous, showing William killing Harold in a man-to-man joust. In fact Harold died on foot, hacked down by the exultant Norman knights as the last of the house-carls fell around him.

10 The last Atheling

1066-1125

DUKE WILLIAM'S HARD-WON VICTORY at Hastings not only deprived the English of their King, it also completed the destruction of the family which had been the leading power in the land for the previous two decades, for both Gyrth and Leofwine Godwinesson died in the battle. Thus neither of Harold's younger brothers survived – like Alfred after the death of Ethelred of Wessex in 871 – to claim the kingship and carry on the fight against the invader. The resultant power vacuum was all the more keenly felt because, in the immediate aftermath of Hastings, the English certainly did not consider themselves a beaten nation. Far from accepting William as king, the Witan in London turned instinctively to the young grandson of Edmund Ironside: the atheling Edgar, last surviving male heir of Alfred's line.

Saxon England had, so to speak, 'been here before'; this was not the first time that the only available heir to the throne had been an untried boy. Edgar was rising fourteen in October 1066, about the same age as his forbears Eadwig, Edgar 'The Peaceable' and Ethelred 'Evil-Counsel' at the beginning of their reigns. The atheling's age did not deter Archbishop Ealdred from proclaiming Edgar king when the grim news of Hastings reached London, and Edwin and Morcar pledged their support. The boy's character, however, proved unequal to the tremendous burden suddenly thrust upon him. Edgar lacked that natural spark of authority which had distinguished Alfred, Edgar 'The Peaceable', and even Edward 'the Confessor' in boyhood. It was not his fault: he had never been groomed for the succession and simply had no idea of how to play the part.

The councillors of the Witan seem to have regretted their impulse almost at once, realizing that they had proclaimed not a confident fledgling ruler, but a bewildered boy. No voice was raised in support of Edgar's immediate coronation. All the tough fighting leaders had been killed at Fulford, Stamford Bridge or Hastings. With no single war-leader of Harold's calibre available to raise a new English army in Edgar's name the Witan dithered helplessly, increasingly aware of its military nakedness as the Norman army began its march on London.

Sensing the hesitancy of the English leaders in London, William decided against a direct advance on the city which might push the English from uncertainty into outright defiance.

After the hunt: an English nobleman begins the ceremonial gutting of the quarry, a deer. Hunting must have been one of Edgar's chief diversions during his long and often humiliating life.

Instead he put on a morale-sapping display of calculated 'frightfulness', marching round London in a wide arc westward through Kent and Surrey, leaving a belt of charred destruction in his army's tracks. Crossing the Thames well to the west of London, William swung in towards the city from the north-west. The Witan followed his approach with all the courage and resolution of sheep being stalked by a circling wolf, and when William reached Berkhamsted the nerve of the English leaders broke at last. From uneasy defiance the Witan's mood slumped into total submission. Taking Edgar with them, the English councillors went out to greet William *en masse* and make their formal peace with the victor of Hastings.

The *Chronicle*, recording the event, struck a note of bitterness mingled with shame:

> There [William] was met by Archbishop Ealdred and Prince Edgar, and Earl Edwin and Earl Morcar, and all the chief men of London. And they submitted out of necessity after most damage had been done – and it was a great piece of folly that they had not done it earlier, since God would not make things better because of our sins. And they gave hostages and swore oaths to him, and he promised to them that he would be a gracious liege lord, and yet in the meantime they ravaged all that they overran.

The most notable feature of the English surrender after Hastings is its completeness – a result, in part, of the new unity which the Danish kings had hammered into the English kingdom. Only fifty years before Hastings, and after a crushing English defeat at Ashingdon, Edmund Ironside and Canute had agreed to partition the realm. In late 1066 the leading lights of the Witan – Ealdred of York, Edwin and Morcar – spoke for the north. They might well have accepted Edgar as king over Northumbria and Mercia and proposed a treaty leaving Wessex and the south to William; the men who had beaten Harold Hardraada in the north could surely have dealt on equal terms with the man who had beaten the Godwinessons in the south. But if such a compromise was ever contemplated after Hastings there is no record of it. Instead the dour realism with which they had accepted Harold as the best man to succeed Edward at the beginning of the year now led the English to reject Edgar, accepting William as the best man to succeed Harold at the end of the year:

> Then on Christmas Day, Archbishop Ealdred consecrated him king at Westminster. And he promised Ealdred on Christ's book and swore moreover (before Ealdred would place the crown on his head) that he would rule all this people as well as the best of the kings before him, *if they would be loyal to him*. [Author's italics].

The crux was William's claim to rule England as the true successor to Edward, and his undertaking to observe the laws and customs of Edward's time. Canute had made a similar promise to rule as the successor to Edgar 'the Peaceable' – but only *after* he had liquidated all the potential leaders of English resistance. Had Canute been the new king in 1066, Edgar the

208

Atheling's chances of dying in bed would have been very doubtful. William, however, realized that the atheling posed no direct personal threat. Courtesy and consideration are not qualities usually associated with William the Conqueror, but as far as the Old English aristocracy was concerned he asked no more than that 'they would be loyal to him'. He was content to 'feather-bed' the magnates of the Witan by allowing them large estates and an honoured status, fully aware of the immense trouble they could make as figureheads of rebellion but

A young English king in the field, surrounded by arguing councillors – precisely Edgar's position during the northern rebellion of 1069–70.

determined to give them a chance to prove their loyalty. As the Old English earls, bishops and abbots died off they could be, and were, replaced by Normans. Here was a policy in total contrast to Canute's purges by assassination and exile fifty years before.

When William returned to Normandy for his first visit to the duchy after Hastings (February-December 1067) he took with him Edgar, Edwin, Morcar, Waltheof (son of Earl Siward), the Abbot of Glastonbury and the contentious Archbishop Stigand. By paying these worthies the high honour of constant attendance at his court, William was of course able to keep an eye on them; but they were certainly not kept under house arrest. In fact William allowed his English guests too much liberty for his own comfort, for in the summer of 1067 Edgar fled the Norman court and headed north across the Channel.

As the Norman hold on England was still virtually confined to the south, Edgar could have triggered a national rising if he had landed in the Humber, got himself crowned king at York and raised the north. But he was still barely fifteen years old and dominated by his mother, the Princess Agatha, a member of the ruling line of the Holy Roman Empire who seems to have been content with escape from the Norman world. Agatha, Edgar, and his sisters Margaret and Christina arrived as refugees at the court of Malcolm Canmore, King of Scotland. Malcolm's courtship and subsequent marriage to Margaret had immense consequences as a civilizing influence in Scotland; but it also gave Edgar a permanent refuge in the north, and the option of Scottish support for any attempt he might care to make on the English throne.

Yet Edgar's utter uselessness as a national leader was demonstrated over the next three terrible years, when Northumbria and Mercia rose in open revolt against William and welcomed Edgar as king. In 1069 the insurgents stormed York and wiped out the Norman garrison there; but this short-lived triumph had been made possible only by inviting a Danish fleet to England. Within four years of Hastings, the leaders of resistance in England had reached the point where they were ready to offer the English crown to Sweyn Estrithson, Canute's nephew, rather than the ineffective Edgar.

The lack of any positive leadership from Edgar led to uncertainties and divisions among the insurgents which William exploited to the hilt by keeping the sources of rebellion isolated and defeating them piecemeal. By the time that William clinched his conquest of the north with his terrible devastation of Yorkshire in the winter of 1069–70, Edgar was safely back in Scotland.

The atheling next surfaced in 1074 when he was approached by Philip, the French king, with an invitation to cross the Channel and harass Normandy from French soil. Although the *Chronicle* makes it clear that this was yet another personal fiasco for Edgar, it is also plain that William was content to buy off the atheling rather than use more drastic measures:

> The king of France, Philip, sent a missive to him and ordered him to come to him saying he would give him the castle of Montreuil so that he could do daily harm to those who were not his friends. So now King Malcolm and Edgar's sister, Margaret, gave him and all his men great gifts and many treasures consisting of skins covered with purple cloth, and robes of marten's skin, and of grey fur, and ermine, and costly robes and golden vessels and silver and led him and all his naval force out of his jurisdiction with great honour. But on the journey it turned out badly for them when they were out at sea, in that they met rough sailing weather, and the raging sea and the strong wind cast them ashore so that all their ships foundered and they themselves got to land with difficulty and their treasure was nearly all lost. And some of his men were captured by the French, but he and his fittest men went back to Scotland, some walking miserably on foot, and some riding wretchedly. Then King Malcolm advised him to send overseas to King William and ask for his protection, and he did so; and the king granted it to him and sent for him. And again King Malcolm and Edgar's sister gave him and all his men immense treasure, and again very honourably sent him out of their jurisdiction. And the sheriff of York came out to meet them at Durham and went all the way with them and had them provided with food and fodder at every castle they came to, until they got overseas to the king. And King William received him with great honour and he stayed there at court and received such dues as were appointed him.

For the last thirteen years of William's reign Edgar seems to have lived in increasing obscurity at the Conqueror's court and on his own modest estates in Normandy. At some stage he must have been knighted, because in 1086 William allowed him to

OVERLEAF Review of the kings of England, from Ethelbert of Kent to William of Normandy.

enirancius due canimbrest
andrager hurreller carlebarno
in regiu̅ z ebu̅ro o̅es illi fue
ru̅e z birta̅nia ad incarnacōm̅
xp̅i reges.

puelu̅ filius eč cu̅ x̅ an̅is
regnasset ab hoc se̅o migrat
in dieb; ei̅ narcus e̅ xp̅s ex
maria u̅gine cui̅ p̅cioso san
gui̅ne humanu̅ gen̅ redemp
tu̅ est.

up̅ denus ebn̅it a̅ roma
nis rotu̅uit. Olaudiu̅ u̅
cōsar bello slu̅ut cu̅ z armi
garu̅ rege starui̅ h̅ hono
re claudu̅ z clau̅ estra̅ funda
tk̅ct.

ru̅gilus indieb;
ap̅ls anuochena̅ ec̅u̅
uit roma̅q̅ inde bou
uit unde ep̅ac̅u̅ z timi
eua̅gliu̅m po̅ticare

Cassianus frem̅ su̅ p̅mog;
interficit z in loca ei̅ regnaui̅

Carausius tira̅nnus oc
cidit bassanu̅ rege z gubna
culu̅ regni tenui̅t

Arctus occidit carau̅sium
rege z sohu̅ regnu̅ suscepit

elepiodocus du̅
ic occidit alectu̅ ro
do̅ne un di̅ mallebu̅
elocra e̅ p̅sc̅no du̅
mp̅atoriu̅ z se̅s Alb
sus e̅ regnaui̅tq̅;

arius astriā cōstruxit et   Coillus filius cyarū reg̃   Lucius hic prius fide xp̄iani   Seuerus imp̄ator ē vē
lapidem in primam eī de uoĉ suā   cepit cōstituitq̄ xx̄viī epos mis   nit britones rebellantes
dā est westmeria crexit mū   tāma + tres archiepos in trib̄ nob   fecit wallū inē briono
in g̃spus cxuiī memoriam eī   liorib; ciuitatib; britanū in deb La   los ac turre a fulgeuci
uꝙ in hodiernū diem res   done ac eboracē + in urbe legi   duĉe picto; ap̄ ebora
tat̃ur nūc i baisata ē hyberū   onū q̄ sic vocari pʒmē edixit fra   cisus est.
                                ta fuit, ubi osca cadit in sabr
                                alle nero in urbe glocestē se
                                pultus est. anno ab incarnacōe
                                E. lo. vii herede caruit.

ole dux colcestē asclepiod   Constantiū senator urbis   Constantin filius eius +   Octauius dux Gew
ini ociait + regni diadema   Rome cole regem subiugāit   sc̄e elene regnauit + postea   ossidit ꝓconsules Ro
te tese insignuit + genuit   ē + post morte eī regnauit   Romā occupauit + monar   ꝙb; regnū insule pʒ
sanctā elenam.   ꝓ annis + elenam sc̄am fil   chiā toci mūdi optinuit.   fuerāt + regni solū pa
                                cole duxit uxore + cū ā rō
                                pʒfilit ipe apud eborachū
                                rei subiacentis

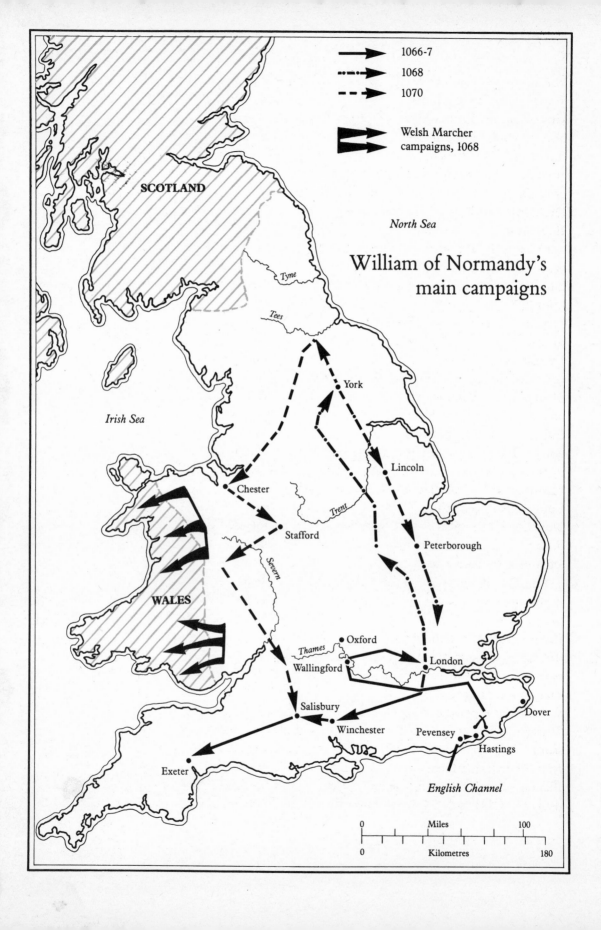

1066-7
1068
1070

Welsh Marcher
campaigns, 1068

SCOTLAND

North Sea

Tyne

Tees

William of Normandy's main campaigns

York

Irish Sea

Lincoln

Chester

Trent

Stafford

Peterborough

Severn

WALES

Thames • Oxford

Wallingford

London

Salisbury

Winchester

Dover

Pevensey

Exeter

Hastings

English Channel

| 0 | | Miles | | 100 |

| 0 | | Kilometres | | 180 |

lead an expedition of 200 knights to Apulia in southern Italy. For that year the *Chronicle* records that 'Prince Edgar, Edward's kinsman, left him [William] because he did not have much honour from him, but may Almighty God grant him honour in the future.' Needless to say, Edgar lost his estates in Normandy after the Conqueror's death in 1087, when his importance as a potential pretender shrank to third place behind Canute II of Denmark and Robert, Duke of Normandy, the Conqueror's eldest son.

In 1091 Edgar was reconciled to the new king, William Rufus, by his part in negotiating a peace between Rufus and King Malcolm of Scotland. As a client of Rufus, Edgar's finest hour came in 1097 when he marched into Scotland at the head of an army, drove out the usurping King Dufenal, and installed his own nephew Edgar on the Scottish throne as a vassal of the English king. This remains the sole positive achievement recorded during Edgar's life and a most ironic role for the head of an ousted royal line to play. After the death of William Rufus and the accession of Henry I, youngest son of the Conqueror, Edgar again ended up on the wrong side during the final confrontation in Normandy between Henry and Duke Robert in 1106. On the fortieth anniversary of Hastings, when a Norman duke had launched the conquest of England, the English king reconquered Normandy in the battle of Tinch-brai. Edgar, needless to say, had thrown in his lot with Duke Robert and was captured by Henry; but 'the King afterwards let him go unmolested'.

Edgar seems to have lived out the rest of his life in Scotland, dying in about 1125. He lived long enough to see yet another pretender eclipse him as the most dangerous claimant to the English throne: William the Clito, son of Duke Robert. A decent, mediocre character who was never big enough for the role demanded of him by history, Edgar the Atheling left no male heir of his own, and with him the line of Alfred the Great – the ancient royal house of Cerdic of Wessex, descendants of Woden – came to an end. But that was not quite the end of the story, for Edgar's niece Edith married Henry I. Their daughter Matilda married Geoffrey of Anjou, and their son was Henry Plantagenet, 'Curtmantle', first of the glorious Plantagenet dynasty which ruled England for over three centuries.

OPPOSITE After William's victory at Hastings there was a period of frightened acquiescence, followed by a violent English reaction in the west (1067), the north (1068), and finally in the west and the north (1069–70). William's response was to reduce all Yorkshire to a blackened, deserted waste.

As for the achievement of the Saxon kings, let Kipling have the last word:

The King's Task

After the sack of the City, when Rome was sunk to a name,
In the years when the Lights were darkened, or ever Saint Wilfred
    came,
Low on the borders of Britain, the ancient poets sing,
Between the cliff and the forest there ruled a Saxon king.

Stubborn all were his people, a stark and a jealous horde –
Not to be schooled by the cudgel, scarce to be cowed by the sword;
Blithe to turn at their pleasure, bitter to cross in their mood,
And set on the ways of their choosing as the hogs of Andred's Wood...

They made them laws in the Witan, the laws of flaying and fine,
Folkland, common and pannage, the theft and the track of kine;
Statutes of tun and of market for the fish and the malt and the meal,
The tax on the Bramber packhorse and the tax on the Hastings keel.
Over the graves of the Druids and over the wreck of Rome
Rudely but deeply they bedded the plinth of the days to come.
Behind the feet of the Legions and before the Northman's ire,
Rudely but greatly begat they the body of state and of shire.
Rudely but greatly they laboured, and their labour stands till now
If we trace on our ancient headlands the twist of their eight-ox plough.

Select bibliography

Reference

Douglas, David C., and Greenaway, George W., eds., *English Historical Documents: Vol.2, 1042–1189* (Eyre & Spottiswoode, 1953)

Stenton, Sir Frank, *Anglo-Saxon England* (Oxford University Press, 1947)

Whitelock, Dorothy, *The Beginnings of English Society* (Penguin, 1952)

Whitelock, Dorothy, ed., *English Historical Documents: Vol. 1, c 500–1042* (Eyre & Spottiswoode, 1953)

General

Barlow, Professor Frank, *Edward the Confessor* (Eyre & Spottiswoode, 1970)

Bede, *A History of the English Church and People* (Penguin Classics, 1955)

Foote, P.G., and Wilson, D.M., *The Viking Achievement* (Sidgwick & Jackson, 1970)

Humble, Richard, *The Fall of Saxon England* (Arthur Barker, 1975)

Loyn, Henry, *The Norman Conquest* (Hutchinson University Library, 1965)

Magnusson, Magnus, *Hammer of the North* (Orbis, 1976)

Magnusson, Magnus, and Palsson, Hermann, *King Harald's Saga* (Penguin Classics, 1966)

Index